THE BIGGEST BANKING SCANDALS

Knowing about the biggest banking scandals can have several advantages, both for individuals and society as a whole. First and foremost, understanding the causes and consequences of these scandals can help individuals protect their own financial interests. By learning from past mistakes, individuals can identify warning signs and avoid investing in companies or financial products that may be risky or fraudulent.

Secondly, studying banking scandals can also inform policy decisions aimed at preventing similar events in the future. Governments, regulators, and industry participants can learn from the failures and weaknesses exposed by these scandals to strengthen regulatory frameworks and corporate governance practices.

Thirdly, awareness of banking scandals can also foster greater transparency and accountability in the financial sector. Increased scrutiny from investors, analysts, and the public can pressure companies to adopt more responsible and ethical business practices, reducing the likelihood of fraudulent or unethical behavior.

Finally, understanding the impacts of banking scandals on the wider economy can help individuals and policymakers anticipate and prepare for potential economic shocks. The collapse of major financial institutions can have far-reaching consequences, including job losses, reduced economic growth, and even recession. By understanding the root causes and systemic risks of these scandals, individuals and governments can take steps to mitigate the impact of future crises.

Written by: A Salt Amazon

Table of Content

Commerzbank Money Laundering Scandal (2020)

BNP Paribas Scandal (2014)

WELLS FARGO ACCOUNT FRAUD SCANDAL (2016)

The Wells Fargo Account Fraud Scandal, also known as the Wells Fargo fake account scandal, was a financial scandal that rocked the banking industry in 2016. It involved one of the largest banks in the United States, Wells Fargo, and its employees' fraudulent creation of unauthorized bank and credit card accounts in the names of existing customers without their knowledge or consent. The scandal was first revealed by the Consumer Financial Protection Bureau (CFPB) and the Office of the Comptroller of the Currency (OCC) on September 8, 2016, and its impact was felt across the industry.

The scandal originated from Wells Fargo's aggressive sales targets and goals, which required employees to cross-sell products to existing customers. The bank's culture fostered a highly competitive environment where employees were pressured to meet unrealistic sales quotas and were incentivized through bonuses and promotions. In order to meet these targets, employees resorted to creating fraudulent accounts, falsifying customer signatures, and using customer data without authorization. The bank's lack of internal controls, oversight, and ethical culture allowed the fraud to continue undetected for years.

The fraud was exposed when the Los Angeles Times published an investigation into the bank's sales practices in 2013, detailing allegations of aggressive sales tactics and unrealistic sales goals. The bank responded by firing around 30 employees. However, the scandal did not come to light until the CFPB, OCC, and the City of Los Angeles announced a settlement with Wells Fargo in September 2016. The bank agreed to pay $185 million in fines and refunds to affected customers.

The revelation of the scandal caused widespread public outrage and scrutiny of Wells Fargo's practices. Customers, shareholders, and lawmakers criticized the bank for its lack of accountability and ethical lapses. The bank's stock price also plummeted, leading to significant financial losses for investors.

The scandal led to a series of leadership changes at Wells Fargo. CEO John Stumpf appeared before the Senate Banking Committee to answer questions about the scandal but faced criticism for blaming low-level employees for the fraud, rather than taking responsibility as the bank's leader. He resigned from his position as CEO, effective immediately, in October 2016. Timothy Sloan, the bank's president and chief operating officer, took over as CEO. The bank also made changes to its board of directors and senior leadership team in the aftermath of the scandal.

The impacts of the scandal were far-reaching. The scandal tarnished Wells Fargo's reputation as a trusted and customer-focused bank. The bank's aggressive sales practices and lack of accountability led to a loss of trust among customers and the general public. The bank faced regulatory scrutiny and was placed under a Federal Reserve enforcement action in 2018. The bank also incurred significant legal costs and reputational damage. The scandal also led to a loss of customers for Wells Fargo, as many customers closed their accounts and switched to other banks.

In response to the scandal, Wells Fargo made significant changes to its sales practices and internal controls. The bank eliminated sales goals for retail bankers, increased training and oversight, and implemented new processes for detecting and preventing fraud. However, the impact of the scandal continued to be felt for years, and the bank is still working to regain the trust of customers and stakeholders.

In conclusion, the Wells Fargo Account Fraud Scandal was a significant event that shook the banking industry in 2016. It highlighted the importance of ethical and customer-focused practices in the banking industry and led to increased regulatory scrutiny and changes in industry practices. The scandal also demonstrated the need for stronger internal controls and oversight to prevent similar incidents in the future. While the impacts of the scandal were significant and long-lasting, it also served as a wake-up call for the banking industry to prioritize customer interests and ethical practices.

The scandal involved Wells Fargo employees opening unauthorized bank and credit card accounts in the names of existing customers without their knowledge or consent. The employees were found to have created these fraudulent accounts in order to meet sales quotas and earn bonuses. It was estimated that as many as 3.5 million accounts were opened without customers' knowledge or consent.

The following is a chronology of events related to the Wells Fargo Account Fraud Scandal:

1. 2011: Wells Fargo sets aggressive sales targets for its employees, with a focus on cross-selling products to existing customers.
2. 2013: The Los Angeles Times publishes an investigation into the bank's sales practices, detailing allegations of aggressive sales tactics and unrealistic sales goals. The bank responds by firing around 30 employees.
3. 2015: The OCC, Wells Fargo's primary regulator, begins investigating the bank's sales practices.
4. September 2016: The CFPB, OCC, and the City of Los Angeles announce a settlement with Wells Fargo over the unauthorized account openings. The bank agrees to pay $185 million in fines and refunds to affected customers.
5. October 2016: Wells Fargo CEO John Stumpf appears before the Senate Banking Committee to answer questions about the scandal. Stumpf faces criticism for blaming low-level employees for the fraud, rather than taking responsibility as the bank's leader.
6. October 2016: Stumpf resigns from his position as CEO, effective immediately. Timothy Sloan, the bank's president and chief operating officer, takes over as CEO.
7. December 2016: Wells Fargo agrees to pay an additional $110 million to settle a class-action lawsuit brought by affected customers.
8. April 2017: Wells Fargo announces that it will claw back an additional $75 million in compensation from former CEO Stumpf and former head of community banking Carrie Tolstedt.

The Wells Fargo Account Fraud Scandal led to widespread public outrage and scrutiny of the bank's sales practices. The scandal also resulted in significant financial and reputational damage for Wells Fargo, as well as regulatory and legal repercussions.

The Wells Fargo Account Fraud Scandal had significant impacts on the bank and its stakeholders. Some of the key impacts of the scandal are:

1. Financial penalties: As a result of the scandal, Wells Fargo was fined $185 million by regulators and agreed to pay an additional $110 million to settle a class-action lawsuit brought by affected customers. The bank also incurred significant legal costs and reputational damage.

2. Reputation damage: The scandal tarnished Wells Fargo's reputation as a trusted and customer-focused bank. The bank's aggressive sales practices and lack of accountability led to a loss of trust among customers and the general public.

3. Leadership changes: The scandal led to the resignation of CEO John Stumpf and the appointment of Timothy Sloan as CEO. The bank also made changes to its board of directors and senior leadership team in the aftermath of the scandal.

4. Regulatory scrutiny: The scandal prompted increased regulatory scrutiny of Wells Fargo's practices and resulted in the bank being placed under a Federal Reserve enforcement action in 2018. The bank also faced increased oversight from the Consumer Financial Protection Bureau, the Office of the Comptroller of the Currency, and other regulators.

5. Loss of customers: The scandal led to a loss of customers for Wells Fargo, as many customers closed their accounts and switched to other banks. The bank's reputation damage also made it difficult to attract new customers.

6. Changes to sales practices: In response to the scandal, Wells Fargo made significant changes to its sales practices and internal controls. The bank eliminated sales goals for retail bankers, increased training and oversight, and implemented new processes for detecting and preventing fraud.

Overall, the Wells Fargo Account Fraud Scandal had a significant impact on the bank's finances, reputation, and operations. The scandal also highlighted the importance of ethical and customer-focused practices in the banking industry.

BARCLAYS LIBOR SCANDAL (2012)

The Barclays LIBOR Scandal of 2012 was one of the most significant financial scandals of recent years. It involved one of the world's largest banks, Barclays, and its manipulation of the London Interbank Offered Rate (LIBOR), a benchmark interest rate used as a reference rate for financial products worldwide. The scandal highlighted the lack of integrity in the banking industry and led to significant legal and regulatory action against Barclays and other banks.

The scandal originated from Barclays' traders' attempts to manipulate the LIBOR rate to benefit their trading positions. The LIBOR rate is set daily by a group of banks based on their estimated borrowing costs. It is used as a benchmark for financial products such as mortgages, loans, and derivatives. Barclays' traders colluded with other banks to submit artificially low or high rates to the LIBOR panel, in order to benefit their positions and increase profits.

The manipulation of the LIBOR rate had far-reaching consequences. It distorted financial markets and led to significant losses for investors who relied on the rate as a reference for financial products. The manipulation also led to a loss of trust in the financial system and raised questions about the integrity of the banking industry.

The scandal was first exposed by a whistleblower in 2008, but it was not until 2012 that the full extent of the manipulation was revealed. In June 2012, Barclays agreed to pay $453 million in fines to regulators in the US and UK for its role in the scandal. The bank also faced significant reputational damage, as its CEO Bob Diamond and other senior executives were forced to resign in the aftermath of the scandal.

The Barclays LIBOR Scandal had significant legal and regulatory consequences. The bank faced investigations by regulators in the US, UK, and other countries, which resulted in fines and legal settlements totaling more than $2.4 billion. Other banks were also implicated in the scandal and faced similar legal action, including UBS, Citigroup, and Deutsche Bank.

The scandal also led to significant regulatory reforms in the banking industry. In the UK, the Financial Conduct Authority (FCA) was established to improve the integrity of financial markets and hold banks accountable for their actions. The FCA imposed stricter regulations on the setting of benchmark interest rates, and banks were required to implement stronger controls and oversight to prevent similar incidents in the future.

The impacts of the Barclays LIBOR Scandal were significant and long-lasting. The scandal highlighted the lack of integrity in the banking industry and raised questions about the effectiveness of regulatory oversight. The scandal also led to a loss of trust in the banking industry, as customers and investors questioned the reliability and accuracy of financial benchmarks.

In response to the scandal, Barclays made significant changes to its leadership and corporate culture. The bank implemented stronger controls and oversight, and its new CEO, Antony Jenkins, announced a "cultural revolution" aimed at rebuilding trust in the bank. However, the impact of the scandal continued to be felt for years, as the bank faced ongoing regulatory scrutiny and legal action.

In conclusion, the Barclays LIBOR Scandal was a significant event that exposed the lack of integrity in the banking industry and led to significant legal and regulatory action. The scandal highlighted the importance of transparency and accountability in the financial system and led to regulatory reforms aimed at improving the integrity of financial benchmarks. While the impacts of the scandal were significant and long-lasting, it also served as a wake-up call for the banking industry to prioritize ethical practices and customer interests.

Chronological order of events related to the Barclays LIBOR Scandal:

1. 2005-2007: Barclays traders begin manipulating the LIBOR rate to benefit their trading positions.
2. 2008: A whistleblower raises concerns about manipulation of the LIBOR rate at Barclays.
3. 2009-2010: Regulators in the US and UK begin investigating allegations of LIBOR manipulation at several banks, including Barclays.
4. April 2012: Barclays is fined £290 million ($450 million) by UK and US regulators for its role in manipulating the LIBOR rate.
5. June 2012: CEO Bob Diamond and other senior executives at Barclays resign in the aftermath of the scandal.
6. July 2012: US and UK regulators release a series of emails and other documents that reveal the extent of the LIBOR manipulation at Barclays.
7. 2012-2014: Barclays faces ongoing regulatory scrutiny and legal action related to the LIBOR scandal, resulting in fines and legal settlements totaling more than $2.4 billion.
8. 2013: UK regulators introduce new rules to improve the setting of benchmark interest rates and prevent future manipulation.
9. 2014: Barclays announces a restructuring plan aimed at improving its financial performance and corporate culture.
10. 2015: Antony Jenkins is ousted as CEO of Barclays amid

concerns about the bank's financial performance and corporate culture.

11. 2017: Barclays and four former executives are charged with fraud related to the bank's fundraising during the 2008 financial crisis. The trial is ongoing.

The Barclays LIBOR Scandal had far-reaching implications for the financial industry and global economy. Some of the wider implications include:

1. Damage to Barclays' Reputation: The scandal seriously damaged Barclays' reputation as a leading financial institution. The bank was widely criticized for its unethical behavior, and its senior executives were forced to resign.

2. Regulatory Crackdown: The scandal led to a regulatory crackdown on the banking industry, with regulators

around the world increasing their oversight and imposing stricter regulations on banks. This included increased scrutiny of benchmark interest rates, such as LIBOR, and tougher penalties for banks found to be engaging in misconduct.

3. Impact on the Financial Industry: The scandal had a wider impact on the financial industry, as it raised concerns about the reliability of benchmark interest rates and the integrity of the financial markets. This led to a loss of confidence among investors and the public, which had a negative impact on the global economy.

4. Legal and Financial Costs: Barclays faced significant legal and financial costs as a result of the scandal. The bank paid fines and legal settlements totaling more than $2.4 billion, and was forced to implement significant reforms to improve its compliance and risk management practices.

5. Increased Scrutiny of Senior Executives: The scandal also led to increased scrutiny of senior executives in the banking industry. In the aftermath of the scandal, several high-profile executives were forced to resign or were dismissed from their positions.

6. Calls for Greater Accountability and Transparency: The scandal highlighted the need for greater accountability and transparency in the banking industry. There were calls for banks to adopt more ethical and responsible practices, and for regulators to strengthen their oversight and enforcement measures to prevent future misconduct.

Overall, the Barclays LIBOR Scandal had a significant impact on the financial industry and global economy. It highlighted the need for greater transparency, accountability, and ethics in the banking industry, and led to increased regulatory oversight and tougher penalties for banks found to be engaging in misconduct.

HSBC MONEY LAUNDERING SCANDAL (2012)

In 2012, allegations emerged that HSBC had been involved in money laundering for several years, specifically that the bank had laundered billions of dollars for Mexican drug cartels and conducted transactions with countries subject to international sanctions, such as Iran and Sudan. These allegations were brought to light after a U.S. Senate investigation found that HSBC had allowed its subsidiaries in Mexico, Saudi Arabia, and Bangladesh to move billions of dollars in suspicious transactions, while ignoring warning signs that the funds might be connected to drug trafficking and other criminal activities.

The Senate report highlighted numerous instances of suspicious transactions that should have been flagged by HSBC's anti-money laundering controls but were not. For example, HSBC Mexico was found to have moved $7 billion in cash transactions from 2007 to 2008, despite the fact that the bank's anti-money laundering unit had identified the branch as a "high risk" for money laundering. The report also revealed that HSBC had failed to properly monitor its correspondent banking relationships, which allowed it to do business with high-risk customers and countries without proper due diligence.

As a result of these findings, HSBC agreed to pay a record $1.9 billion in fines to U.S. authorities and implement various reforms to strengthen its anti-money laundering controls. The bank also had to enter into a five-year deferred prosecution agreement with the U.S. Department of Justice, meaning that if HSBC failed to comply with the terms of the agreement, criminal charges could be filed against the bank.

The scandal led to the resignation of the bank's CEO at the time, Stuart Gulliver, and damaged HSBC's reputation as a global financial institution. In response, the bank launched a major restructuring effort to improve its compliance culture and reduce its exposure to high-risk countries and customers.

The HSBC money laundering scandal of 2012 was one of the largest and most damaging to hit the banking industry in recent years. It highlighted the need for banks to strengthen their anti-money laundering controls and reminded regulators and law enforcement agencies of the importance of holding financial institutions accountable for their actions.

Background

HSBC is a British multinational banking and financial services company. In the early 2000s, HSBC began to expand its presence in Mexico and the United States, particularly in the areas of correspondent banking and remittances. Correspondent banking involves one bank providing services to another bank in a different country, such as wire transfers and foreign currency transactions. Remittances involve the transfer of money by foreign workers to their families in their home countries.

Chronology of Events

1. 2006-2007: HSBC begins acquiring Mexican banks and begins to increase its correspondent banking activities in Mexico.
2. 2008: The US Office of the Comptroller of the Currency (OCC) issues a cease-and-desist order to HSBC for its poor anti-money laundering controls.
3. 2008-2010: HSBC's compliance department begins to raise concerns about potential money laundering risks

in Mexico and the bank's failure to properly monitor its correspondent banking activities.

4. 2010-2012: The US Senate Permanent Subcommittee on Investigations conducts an investigation into HSBC's compliance with anti-money laundering regulations and its relationship with Mexican drug cartels and Iranian banks. The investigation reveals that HSBC had processed billions of dollars in transactions for Mexican drug cartels and had violated US sanctions against Iran. The investigation also reveals that HSBC had ignored warnings from its compliance department and had failed to properly monitor its correspondent banking activities.

5. July 2012: The US Senate Permanent Subcommittee on Investigations releases a report on its findings, accusing HSBC of being a "pervasively polluted" institution that had facilitated money laundering for drug cartels and terrorist organizations.

6. December 2012: HSBC agrees to pay a $1.92 billion fine to settle the charges against it. The bank also agrees to enter into a deferred prosecution agreement with the US Department of Justice, which requires the bank to improve its anti-money laundering and sanctions compliance programs and submit to ongoing monitoring by an independent compliance monitor.

Impacts

The HSBC money laundering scandal had significant impacts on the bank and the wider financial industry.

1. Reputational Damage: The scandal severely damaged HSBC's reputation and raised concerns about the bank's compliance and risk management practices.

2. Legal and Financial Costs: HSBC paid a $1.92 billion fine to settle the charges against it, one of the largest penalties ever levied against a financial institution. The bank also incurred significant legal and compliance costs as a result of the scandal.

3. Regulatory Scrutiny: The scandal led to increased regulatory scrutiny of the banking industry, particularly in the areas of anti-money laundering and

sanctions compliance. Regulators around the world began to impose stricter regulations and penalties on banks found to be engaging in misconduct.

4. Impact on the Financial Industry: The scandal had a wider impact on the financial industry, as it raised concerns about the integrity of the financial system and the effectiveness of anti-money laundering and sanctions compliance measures.

5. Calls for Greater Accountability and Transparency: The scandal highlighted the need for greater accountability and transparency in the banking industry. There were calls for banks to adopt more ethical and responsible practices, and for regulators to strengthen their oversight and enforcement measures to prevent future misconduct.

Overall, the HSBC money laundering scandal of 2012 was a significant event in the history of the banking industry. It exposed the risks and consequences of failing to properly manage money laundering and sanctions compliance risks, and led to increased regulatory scrutiny and tougher penalties for banks found to be engaging in misconduct.

JPMORGAN CHASE LONDON WHALE SCANDAL (2012)

The JPMorgan Chase London Whale scandal was a major event in the financial industry that occurred in 2012. It involved the bank's Chief Investment Office (CIO) taking on a large portfolio of complex financial instruments, primarily credit derivatives, to protect the bank against credit risk. The portfolio grew to become one of the largest in the market, worth approximately $350 billion by 2011, but it also became increasingly complex and difficult to manage. In early 2012, the CIO began to experience significant losses in the portfolio, which led to media reports about a large and mysterious trading position at JPMorgan's London office.

The losses were initially downplayed by the bank's CEO, Jamie Dimon, but it later became clear that the losses were much larger than originally estimated and that the bank had not properly disclosed the risks associated with the trades. The scandal resulted in JPMorgan losing over $6 billion on the trades, making it one of the largest trading losses in history, and the bank was fined $920 million by various regulators for failing to properly manage the risks associated with the trades.

The incident led to increased calls for tighter regulation of the financial industry and raised questions about the efficacy of the so-called "Volcker Rule," a provision of the Dodd-Frank financial reform law that was designed to restrict banks from making risky trades with their own money.

Background:

JPMorgan's CIO was responsible for managing the bank's excess deposits and making investments to generate additional revenue. In 2006, the CIO began investing in a portfolio of synthetic credit derivatives that was designed to protect the bank against credit risk. These derivatives were essentially bets on whether a basket of companies would default on their debt.

The portfolio grew to become one of the largest positions in the market, and by 2011 it was worth approximately $350 billion. However, it also became increasingly complex and difficult to manage, and by early 2012, the CIO began to experience significant losses in the portfolio.

The Scandal:

In April 2012, media reports began to emerge about a large and mysterious trading position at JPMorgan's London office. The reports suggested that the bank had taken on a massive bet on credit derivatives that had gone wrong, leading to losses that could exceed $2 billion.

Initially, JPMorgan downplayed the losses, with CEO Jamie Dimon dismissing them as a "tempest in a teapot." However, as more information came to light, it became clear that the losses were much larger than originally estimated and that the bank had not properly disclosed the risks associated with the trades.

It was later revealed that the CIO had taken on massive positions in credit default swaps, which are essentially insurance policies that pay out if a company defaults on its debt. The trades were so large that they were distorting the market, and other traders began to bet against JPMorgan, exacerbating the losses.

The Aftermath:

As the losses continued to mount, JPMorgan was forced to unwind the trades and take massive write-downs. In total, the bank lost over $6 billion on the trades, making it one of the largest trading losses in history.

The scandal led to significant regulatory scrutiny of JPMorgan, and the bank was fined $920 million by various regulators for failing to properly manage the risks associated with the trades. Several executives at the bank, including Bruno Iksil, were also fired or forced to resign in the aftermath of the scandal.

The incident also led to increased calls for tighter regulation of the financial industry and raised questions about the efficacy of the so-called "Volcker Rule," a provision of the Dodd-Frank financial reform law that was designed to restrict banks from making risky trades with their own money.

Key events that occurred during the JPMorgan Chase London Whale scandal:

1. In 2006, JPMorgan's Chief Investment Office (CIO) began investing in a portfolio of synthetic credit derivatives to protect the bank against credit risk.
2. By 2011, the portfolio had grown to approximately $350 billion and had become increasingly complex and difficult to manage.
3. In early 2012, the CIO began to experience significant losses in the portfolio.
4. In April 2012, media reports emerged about a large and mysterious trading position at JPMorgan's London office.
5. The bank initially downplayed the losses, with CEO Jamie Dimon dismissing them as a "tempest in a teapot."
6. However, it later became clear that the losses were much larger than originally estimated and that the bank had not properly disclosed the risks associated with the trades.
7. The CIO had taken on massive positions in credit default swaps, which were distorting the market, and other traders began to bet against JPMorgan, exacerbating the losses.
8. The losses continued to mount, and JPMorgan was forced to unwind the trades and take massive write-downs.
9. In total, the bank lost over $6 billion on the trades, making it one of the largest trading losses in history.
10. JPMorgan was fined $920 million by various regulators for failing to properly manage the risks associated with the trades.
11. Several executives at the bank, including Bruno Iksil (the trader known as "the London Whale"), were fired or forced to resign in the aftermath of the scandal.
12. The incident led to increased calls for tighter regulation of the financial industry and raised questions about the efficacy of the so-called "Volcker Rule," a provision of the Dodd-Frank financial reform law that was designed to

restrict banks from making risky trades with their own money.

In the end, the London Whale scandal served as a cautionary tale about the dangers of complex financial instruments and the need for greater transparency and oversight in the banking industry.

GOLDMAN SACHS ABACUS MORTGAGE SCANDAL (2010)

The Goldman Sachs Abacus Mortgage scandal was a major event in the financial industry that occurred in 2010. It involved the creation and marketing of a complex financial instrument called a synthetic collateralized debt obligation (CDO) known as Abacus.

Goldman Sachs created Abacus in 2007, at the height of the U.S. housing market bubble, as a way to profit from the subprime mortgage market. The CDO was made up of a pool of residential mortgage-backed securities (RMBS) that were underwritten by Goldman Sachs and sold to investors. The CDO was structured so that investors could bet on the performance of the RMBS, with different tranches having different levels of risk and return.

The scandal arose when it was discovered that Goldman Sachs had marketed and sold Abacus to investors without disclosing that a hedge fund, Paulson & Co., had played a significant role in selecting the underlying assets for the CDO. Paulson & Co. had taken a short position on the CDO, meaning that they would profit if the CDO performed poorly. This created a conflict of interest, as Goldman Sachs was marketing the CDO as a good investment while Paulson & Co. was betting against it.

The Securities and Exchange Commission (SEC) launched an investigation into the matter, and in 2010, Goldman Sachs settled with the SEC for $550 million. As part of the settlement, Goldman

Sachs admitted to making a mistake in not disclosing the role that Paulson & Co. had played in selecting the underlying assets for Abacus.

1. In 2007, Goldman Sachs creates a synthetic collateralized debt obligation (CDO) called Abacus, which is made up of residential mortgage-backed securities (RMBS).
2. Goldman Sachs markets and sells Abacus to investors, with different tranches having different levels of risk and return.
3. Hedge fund Paulson & Co. takes a significant role in selecting the underlying assets for Abacus and takes a short position on the CDO, meaning they will profit if the CDO performs poorly.
4. Goldman Sachs does not disclose the role that Paulson & Co. played in selecting the underlying assets for Abacus to investors.
5. In 2008, the U.S. housing market collapses, and the RMBS underlying Abacus suffer significant losses.
6. In 2009, the Securities and Exchange Commission (SEC) begins an investigation into the marketing and sale of Abacus.
7. In 2010, the SEC charges Goldman Sachs with fraud related to Abacus and its failure to disclose Paulson & Co.'s role in selecting the underlying assets for the CDO.
8. Goldman Sachs settles with the SEC for $550 million and admits to making a mistake in not disclosing the role that Paulson & Co. played in selecting the underlying assets for Abacus.
9. Several Goldman Sachs executives, including Fabrice Tourre, a vice president at the firm who had played a key role in creating and marketing Abacus, face legal and regulatory action.
10. The scandal leads to increased scrutiny of the investment banking industry and increased calls for

tighter regulation and greater transparency in the industry.

The scandal had significant implications for the financial industry, as it raised questions about the ethics of the investment banking industry and the level of disclosure that is required when marketing complex financial instruments. The incident also led to increased scrutiny of the role that investment banks played in the 2008 financial crisis and to increased calls for tighter regulation of the industry.

Goldman Sachs faced significant reputational damage in the aftermath of the scandal, and several executives, including Fabrice Tourre, a vice president at the firm who had played a key role in creating and marketing Abacus, faced legal and regulatory action. The scandal also led to a decline in the profitability of the firm's fixed income division, which had been a major source of revenue for Goldman Sachs prior to the financial crisis.

Reputational damage: The scandal had a significant impact on Goldman Sachs' reputation, as it highlighted the ethical concerns surrounding the investment banking industry and the level of transparency that is required when marketing complex financial instruments.

1. Regulatory changes: The scandal led to increased scrutiny of the investment banking industry and to changes in regulation aimed at increasing transparency and reducing the risk of conflicts of interest. In the aftermath of the scandal, the SEC and other regulatory bodies introduced new rules and regulations, including the Dodd-Frank Wall Street Reform and Consumer Protection Act, which aimed to improve transparency and accountability in the financial industry.

2. Legal and regulatory action: Several Goldman Sachs executives, including Fabrice Tourre, faced legal and regulatory action in the aftermath of the scandal. Tourre was found liable for securities fraud in 2013 and

was ordered to pay a $825,000 fine.

3. Decline in profitability: The scandal also had financial implications for Goldman Sachs, as the firm's fixed income division, which had been a major source of revenue prior to the financial crisis, saw a decline in profitability in the aftermath of the scandal.

4. Increased scrutiny of investment banks' roles in the 2008 financial crisis: The scandal also led to increased scrutiny of the role that investment banks played in the 2008 financial crisis. The Abacus CDO was created at the height of the U.S. housing market bubble, and the scandal raised questions about the extent to which investment banks contributed to the financial crisis.

5. Calls for greater transparency: The scandal also led to increased calls for greater transparency in the investment banking industry, particularly when it comes to complex financial instruments. The incident highlighted the need for greater disclosure and transparency to ensure that investors are fully informed about the risks and benefits associated with these.

Overall, the Goldman Sachs Abacus Mortgage scandal was a significant event in the financial industry that highlighted the risks associated with complex financial instruments and the importance of transparency and disclosure in the investment banking industry. It led to increased scrutiny of the industry and to changes in regulation aimed at increasing transparency and reducing the risk of conflicts of interest.

STANDARD CHARTERED MONEY LAUNDERING SCANDAL (2012)

The Standard Chartered Money Laundering Scandal of 2012 involved allegations of the bank violating U.S. sanctions on Iran by handling hundreds of billions of dollars of transactions for Iranian clients between 2001 and 2007. The scandal led to significant reputational damage for Standard Chartered and raised concerns about the effectiveness of financial regulations and oversight in preventing money laundering and other illegal activities.

The allegations against Standard Chartered were first made public in August 2012 when the New York State Department of Financial Services (DFS) released a statement accusing the bank of concealing around 60,000 transactions with Iranian clients that amounted to at least $250 billion. According to the DFS, the bank had deliberately stripped identifying information from the transactions in order to avoid detection by U.S. authorities.

In response to the allegations, Standard Chartered initially denied any wrongdoing and claimed that the transactions in question complied with all relevant regulations. However, as the evidence mounted against the bank, Standard Chartered eventually agreed to a settlement with U.S. authorities in December 2012.

Under the terms of the settlement, Standard Chartered agreed to pay a total of $667 million in fines and penalties to various U.S. authorities, including the DFS, the U.S. Treasury Department, and the Federal Reserve. The bank also agreed to implement a number of measures aimed at improving its compliance procedures and preventing similar violations in the future.

The key events in the Standard Chartered Money Laundering Scandal of 2012:

1. August 6, 2012: The New York State Department of Financial Services (DFS) accuses Standard Chartered of violating U.S. sanctions on Iran by handling around 60,000 transactions with Iranian clients between 2001 and 2007, worth at least $250 billion.

2. August 7, 2012: Standard Chartered denies any wrongdoing and claims that the transactions in question were compliant with all relevant regulations.

3. August 14, 2012: The DFS accuses Standard Chartered of concealing the identifying information of the Iranian transactions in order to avoid detection by U.S. authorities.

4. August 15, 2012: Standard Chartered's share price drops significantly following the allegations.

5. August 17, 2012: The U.S. Treasury Department, Federal Reserve, and other authorities announce that they will also investigate Standard Chartered's compliance with U.S. sanctions on Iran.

6. August 30, 2012: Standard Chartered hires law firm Sullivan & Cromwell to represent it in negotiations with U.S. authorities.

7. December 10, 2012: Standard Chartered agrees to pay a total of $667 million in fines and penalties to various U.S. authorities to settle the allegations. The bank also agrees to implement a number of measures aimed at improving its compliance procedures and preventing similar violations in the future.

8. December 11, 2012: Standard Chartered's CEO, Peter Sands, apologizes for the bank's conduct and acknowledges that it fell short of its own standards and the expectations of regulators and the public.
9. December 19, 2012: Standard Chartered's share price rebounds following the settlement announcement.
10. December 2014: Standard Chartered is fined an additional $300 million by New York's banking regulator for failing to improve its anti-money laundering controls sufficiently after the 2012 scandal.
11. August 2019: Standard Chartered announces that it will pay a total of $1.1 billion to settle allegations by U.S. and U.K. authorities that it violated sanctions on Iran, Sudan, and Syria between 2007 and 2014.

The fallout from the scandal was significant, both for Standard Chartered and for the wider financial industry. The bank suffered a significant drop in its share price following the allegations, and its reputation was tarnished by the perception that it had been involved in illegal activities. The scandal also raised concerns about the effectiveness of financial regulations and oversight, particularly with regard to preventing money laundering and other forms of financial crime.

In response to the scandal, regulators around the world stepped up their efforts to combat money laundering and other illegal activities. In the years since the scandal, there have been a number of high-profile cases involving allegations of money laundering and other financial crimes, including the 1MDB scandal and the recent FinCEN Files revelations.

1. Damage to Reputation: The scandal damaged Standard Chartered's reputation as a trusted and responsible financial institution, which could make it more difficult for the bank to attract and retain customers in the future.

2. Regulatory Scrutiny: The scandal drew increased regulatory scrutiny of the banking industry and prompted calls for tighter controls and tougher enforcement of anti-money laundering laws.

3. Impact on Share Price: Standard Chartered's share price dropped significantly following the allegations, which highlights how much damage a scandal can do to a company's value.

4. Global Political Impact: The scandal prompted diplomatic tensions between the U.S. and U.K. and raised questions about the effectiveness of international sanctions against countries like Iran.

5. Increased Fines and Penalties: The scandal led to increased fines and penalties for banks that violate anti-money laundering laws, which could make it more expensive for banks to operate and may force some smaller banks out of business.

6. Regulatory Overhaul: The scandal contributed to a broader regulatory overhaul of the banking industry, including the creation of the Financial Conduct Authority (FCA) in the UK and increased scrutiny of banks' risk management and compliance procedures.

7. Corporate Governance: The scandal highlighted the importance of good corporate governance and the need for companies to have effective risk management and compliance programs in place.

8. Increased Focus on Culture and Ethics: The scandal helped to focus attention on the importance of corporate culture and ethics in preventing financial misconduct, and prompted calls for more ethical and values-driven banking practices.

Overall, the Standard Chartered Money Laundering Scandal highlighted the need for greater transparency and accountability in the financial industry, as well as the importance of effective regulatory oversight in preventing illegal activities. While significant progress has been made in recent years to improve compliance procedures and combat financial crime, the incident served as a stark reminder of the challenges that remain in ensuring a safe and secure financial system for all.

BANK OF AMERICA MORTGAGE FRAUD SCANDAL (2014)

The Bank of America Mortgage Fraud Scandal (2014) involved allegations that the bank had sold risky mortgage-backed securities to investors without adequately disclosing the risks involved. The scandal ultimately led to a multi-billion dollar settlement with the U.S. government and a significant blow to the bank's reputation.

The origins of the scandal can be traced back to the housing bubble of the mid-2000s. During this time, many banks and financial institutions began packaging and selling subprime mortgages into securities, which they then sold to investors. These securities were often backed by pools of thousands of individual mortgages, many of which were made to borrowers who were unlikely to be able to repay their loans.

In the case of Bank of America, the bank had acquired mortgage lender Countrywide Financial in 2008, just as the housing market was beginning to collapse. Countrywide had been one of the largest originators of subprime mortgages in the U.S., and many of its loans were already in default or on the verge of default when Bank of America acquired it.

Despite this, Bank of America continued to sell mortgage-backed securities to investors, often without fully disclosing the risks involved. Many of these securities were rated as high-quality investments by ratings agencies, despite the fact that they contained large numbers of subprime loans that were already in default.

In 2013, the U.S. government sued Bank of America for allegedly misleading investors about the quality of the mortgage-backed securities it was selling. The government claimed that the bank had concealed information about the risks associated with these securities, and had knowingly sold them to investors who were unlikely to be able to recoup their losses.

In March 2014, Bank of America agreed to a $9.5 billion settlement with the U.S. government to resolve the allegations. This settlement included $6.3 billion in cash payments and $3.2 billion in mortgage relief for borrowers who had been affected by the bank's actions. The settlement was one of the largest ever reached between a bank and the U.S. government.

Chronological list of key events related to the Bank of America Mortgage Fraud Scandal in 2014:

1. March 2014 - Bank of America agrees to a $9.5 billion settlement with the U.S. government to resolve allegations of mortgage fraud related to the sale of mortgage-backed securities between 2005 and 2007.
2. The settlement includes $6.3 billion in cash payments to the government and $3.2 billion in mortgage relief to borrowers who were affected by the bank's actions.
3. The settlement is one of the largest ever reached between a bank and the U.S. government.
4. Bank of America admits no wrongdoing as part of the settlement.
5. The settlement resolves investigations by the U.S. Department of Justice and several state attorneys general into the bank's role in the subprime mortgage crisis.
6. The U.S. government alleges that Bank of America misled investors about the quality of the mortgage-

backed securities it was selling, and concealed information about the risks associated with these securities.

7. The government claims that Bank of America knowingly sold these securities to investors who were unlikely to be able to recoup their losses.
8. The settlement leads to increased regulatory scrutiny of banks and financial institutions, and contributes to the passage of the Dodd-Frank Wall Street Reform and Consumer Protection Act in 2010.
9. Bank of America's reputation and bottom line are significantly impacted by the scandal, with the bank forced to pay out billions of dollars in fines and settlements, and its share price dropping significantly in the wake of the allegations.
10. The scandal also damages the bank's relationships with investors, customers, and regulators, and leads to calls for greater accountability and transparency in the banking industry.

The Bank of America Mortgage Fraud Scandal had far-reaching implications for the banking industry and the broader economy. It highlighted the dangers of subprime lending and the need for greater transparency and accountability in the financial sector. The scandal also led to increased regulatory scrutiny of banks and financial institutions, and contributed to the passage of the Dodd-Frank Wall Street Reform and Consumer Protection Act in 2010, which aimed to prevent a repeat of the 2008 financial crisis.

1. Legal repercussions: Bank of America faced significant legal penalties and settlements related to the scandal, which impacted its financial position and reputation.
2. Increased regulation: The scandal, along with other cases of mortgage fraud and financial misconduct, led to increased regulatory scrutiny and calls for more oversight of financial institutions.
3. Consumer protection: The scandal highlighted the

importance of protecting consumers from predatory lending practices and the need for better education and awareness about mortgages and financial products.

4. Economic impact: The collapse of the housing market and the widespread mortgage fraud contributed to the 2008 financial crisis, which had a significant impact on the global economy and resulted in widespread job losses and economic hardship.

5. Industry-wide changes: The scandal led to changes in the mortgage industry, including increased scrutiny of mortgage applications and stricter lending standards to prevent fraud.

6. Corporate responsibility: The Bank of America scandal raised questions about corporate responsibility and the need for companies to prioritize ethical behavior and compliance with laws and regulations.

For Bank of America, the scandal had a significant impact on the bank's reputation and bottom line. The bank was forced to pay out billions of dollars in fines and settlements, and its share price dropped significantly in the wake of the allegations. The scandal also damaged the bank's relationships with investors, customers, and regulators, and led to calls for greater accountability and transparency in the banking industry.

CITIGROUP ENRON SCANDAL (2002)

The Citigroup Enron scandal of 2002 was a high-profile case of financial misconduct that involved allegations of conflicts of interest and fraudulent financial transactions between the financial services company Citigroup and the energy company Enron. The scandal revealed serious flaws in the financial industry and led to significant legal action, regulatory investigations, and changes in the financial industry.

At the heart of the Citigroup Enron scandal was a series of financial transactions between Citigroup and Enron that allowed Enron to manipulate its financial statements and hide its true financial condition. Citigroup, which had a long-standing relationship with Enron, helped the energy company set up off-balance-sheet entities that were used to hide Enron's debt and inflate its earnings. These off-balance-sheet entities were created by Enron's CFO, Andrew Fastow, who worked closely with Citigroup's structured finance unit to design the transactions.

One of the key transactions at the center of the Citigroup Enron scandal was the creation of a special-purpose entity (SPE) called "Delta" that was used to conceal Enron's losses from its investors. Citigroup invested $375 million in Delta, and in return, Delta issued Citigroup notes that paid interest at a higher rate than Citigroup was paying on its own debt. This allowed Enron to record a gain on its books, even though the transaction had no economic substance.

The SPE Delta was a Special Purpose Entity (SPE) established by Citigroup in 1999 to conduct transactions with Enron. The role of SPE Delta was to allow Enron to transfer assets and liabilities off its balance sheet, thereby reducing Enron's reported debt and making its financial position appear stronger than it actually was.

SPE Delta was used to conduct a number of transactions with Enron, including the purchase of an interest in a Nigerian power plant project, and the sale of Enron stock options. These transactions were structured in such a way that they allowed Enron to report revenue and profits from the transactions, while at the same time hiding losses and debt.

SPE Delta was able to hide Enron's losses because it was an off-balance-sheet entity, meaning that its financial transactions did not have to be reported on Enron's financial statements. Enron's use of SPE Delta allowed it to keep its debt levels hidden from investors and regulators, which helped to prop up its stock price and maintain investor confidence.

The use of SPEs like SPE Delta in the Enron scandal was controversial because it allowed companies to engage in off-balance-sheet financing and accounting, which could be used to hide losses and manipulate financial results. In the aftermath of the scandal, new regulations were put in place to increase transparency and oversight of SPEs and other off-balance-sheet entities.

In addition to these financial transactions, Citigroup was also accused of conflicts of interest in its relationship with Enron. Specifically, Citigroup was alleged to have engaged in investment banking activities for Enron while at the same time providing lending and other financial services to the energy company. This raised questions about whether Citigroup was acting in the best interests of its clients or its own bottom line.

1. 1997-2001: Enron uses complex accounting methods to inflate profits and hide losses, leading to a false impression of its financial health.

2. October 2001: Enron reveals that it has overstated earnings by $600 million over the past five years.

3. November 2001: Enron files for bankruptcy protection, becoming one of the largest corporate bankruptcies in history.

4. December 2001: Citigroup agrees to pay $120 million to settle allegations of helping Enron hide debt.

5. February 2002: The U.S. Securities and Exchange Commission (SEC) launches an investigation into Citigroup's involvement in Enron's fraudulent accounting practices.

6. April 2002: The SEC announces that it is suing Citigroup for its role in Enron's accounting fraud.

7. May 2002: Citigroup agrees to pay $2 billion to settle the SEC's charges that it helped Enron engage in accounting fraud.

8. October 2002: Citigroup agrees to pay $120 million to settle class-action lawsuits brought by Enron shareholders.

9. December 2002: Citigroup agrees to pay $250 million to settle charges that it helped WorldCom, another company embroiled in an accounting scandal, engage in fraudulent accounting practices.

10. 2003-2004: Citigroup agrees to pay additional settlements totaling $2.5 billion to resolve claims related to Enron, WorldCom, and other accounting scandals.

The Citigroup Enron scandal led to significant legal and regulatory action. In 2003, Citigroup agreed to pay $2 billion to settle charges that it helped Enron manipulate its financial statements. The settlement, which was one of the largest ever in a securities fraud case, included payments to Enron investors, as well as changes to Citigroup's business practices. The settlement also led to the creation of an Enron Trust that was funded by the settlement proceeds and used to compensate victims of the fraud.

The scandal also led to increased regulatory scrutiny of the financial industry. In the wake of the Enron collapse and other corporate scandals, Congress passed the Sarbanes-Oxley Act of 2002, which established new requirements for public companies and their auditors, including the creation of an independent oversight board for auditors. This regulatory reform aimed to improve transparency and accountability in the financial industry and restore public confidence in the markets.

The Citigroup Enron scandal highlighted the need for greater transparency and accountability in the financial industry. It demonstrated the dangers of conflicts of interest and the importance of maintaining ethical standards in financial transactions. The scandal also led to changes in the way financial institutions do business and the increased scrutiny of financial transactions that may be used to manipulate financial statements. Overall, the Citigroup Enron scandal had far-reaching consequences for the financial industry and has had a lasting impact on financial regulation and oversight.

BCCI FRAUD SCANDAL (1991)

The Bank of Credit and Commerce International (BCCI) was founded in 1972 by a Pakistani financier named Agha Hasan Abedi. From the outset, the bank was known for its aggressive expansion and unconventional business practices. BCCI grew rapidly by acquiring other banks and businesses around the world and developed a reputation for catering to wealthy clients who wanted to avoid taxes, regulations, or scrutiny from law enforcement agencies.

BCCI's expansion was fueled by its ability to evade banking regulations and oversight. The bank created a network of shell companies and offshore accounts that it used to conceal its true ownership and control. BCCI's lack of transparency allowed it to engage in a variety of illegal activities, including money laundering for drug traffickers and terrorists, falsifying financial statements, bribing government officials, and concealing the true ownership of assets.

One of the key players in the BCCI scandal was a Saudi businessman named Ghaith Pharaon, who owned a significant stake in the bank and was suspected of having links to terrorist organizations. Pharaon was able to evade law enforcement and regulatory scrutiny for years by using a network of shell companies and bank accounts to conceal his ownership and control of BCCI.

Another important figure in the scandal was Agha Hasan Abedi, the founder of BCCI. Abedi was known for his flamboyant lifestyle and his willingness to engage in risky and unconventional business practices. Abedi was accused of masterminding many of the fraudulent activities at BCCI, and he was indicted on charges of money laundering and fraud shortly before his death in 1995.

The fraud at BCCI involved a complex web of transactions and illegal activities, many of which were carried out through a network of shell companies and offshore accounts. The bank's activities were finally exposed in 1991 when regulators in several countries shut down the bank due to allegations of money laundering, bribery, and fraud.

1. 1972: The Bank of Credit and Commerce International (BCCI) is founded by Pakistani financier Agha Hasan Abedi.

2. 1980s: BCCI grows rapidly, expanding into over 70 countries and becoming known for its unconventional business practices and catering to wealthy clients who wanted to avoid taxes, regulations, or scrutiny from law enforcement agencies.

3. 1988: BCCI's activities come under scrutiny when it is accused of fraud and money laundering in a case involving a financial institution in the United Arab Emirates.

4. 1990: Regulators in the United Kingdom, the United States, and other countries begin investigating BCCI's activities.

5. July 1991: Regulators in the United States and the United Kingdom shut down BCCI after uncovering evidence of massive fraud and illegal activities. The bank is later found to have engaged in a variety of illegal practices, including money laundering for drug traffickers and terrorists, falsifying financial statements, bribing government officials, and concealing the true ownership of assets.

6. 1992: BCCI's liquidators file a $10 billion lawsuit against

a number of parties, including Price Waterhouse, the accounting firm that audited the bank's financial statements.

7. 1995: Agha Hasan Abedi, the founder of BCCI, dies shortly before he is due to stand trial on charges of money laundering and fraud.

8. 1998: The liquidators of BCCI reach a settlement with Price Waterhouse, which agrees to pay $195 million in damages.

9. 2005: A report by the U.S. Senate Subcommittee on Investigations concludes that BCCI was involved in a range of illegal activities, including money laundering, drug trafficking, and arms smuggling.

The BCCI scandal had a far-reaching impact on the global financial system. The scandal exposed the weaknesses and vulnerabilities of international banking regulations and oversight. The scandal prompted a wave of regulatory reforms, including the creation of new anti-money laundering laws, the strengthening of banking regulations, and the establishment of international bodies to monitor and regulate financial institutions.

In the aftermath of the BCCI scandal, many questions were raised about the effectiveness of international banking regulations and the ability of regulators to detect and prevent financial fraud. The scandal highlighted the need for greater transparency and oversight in the financial sector and led to significant reforms that helped to strengthen the integrity and stability of the global financial system.

In conclusion, the BCCI fraud scandal was a watershed moment in the history of international banking, and it revealed the dangers of unchecked greed, corruption, and illegal activities in the financial sector. The scandal served as a wake-up call for regulators and policymakers, and it led to significant reforms that helped to strengthen the integrity and stability of the global financial system.

LEHMAN BROTHERS ACCOUNTING FRAUD SCANDAL (2008)

Lehman Brothers was a global financial services firm that was founded in 1850 and had a long history of success and innovation. However, in the early 2000s, Lehman Brothers began to take on greater risks and engage in increasingly complex financial transactions. These actions ultimately led to the firm's collapse in 2008 and one of the most significant financial scandals in history.

The accounting fraud at Lehman Brothers began in the early 2000s when the firm began to engage in a practice known as "repo 105." Repo 105 was a type of short-term financing transaction that allowed Lehman Brothers to temporarily remove assets from its balance sheet and thereby reduce its reported leverage ratio. By removing assets from its balance sheet, Lehman Brothers was able to make its financial position appear stronger and more stable than it actually was.

Here's how it worked:

1. Lehman Brothers would transfer assets, such as securities or bonds, to a counterparty, such as a bank or hedge fund.
2. The counterparty would provide Lehman Brothers with cash for the assets, usually at a discount to their market value.
3. Lehman Brothers would use the cash to pay down debt,

thereby reducing their leverage ratio and improving their financial statements.

4. At the end of the quarter, Lehman Brothers would repurchase the assets from the counterparty, typically at a slightly higher price than the initial sale price.

5. Lehman Brothers would then record the repurchase as a sale in its financial statements, and the cash received would be reported as a reduction in debt.

The key to the repo 105 transaction was that it allowed Lehman Brothers to classify the sale of the assets as a "true sale" for accounting purposes, meaning that the assets would be removed from their balance sheet entirely. This classification allowed Lehman Brothers to temporarily reduce their leverage ratio and make their financial statements appear stronger.

However, it's important to note that repo 105 transactions were not considered fraudulent under generally accepted accounting principles (GAAP) at the time. The issue with Lehman Brothers' use of repo 105 was that it was allegedly used to mislead investors and creditors about the true state of the firm's financial health. The transactions were also reportedly misclassified and used more extensively than was disclosed to regulators and investors, which ultimately contributed to the firm's collapse.

Lehman Brothers' use of repo 105 transactions was highly problematic because it was not transparent and did not accurately reflect the true financial position of the firm. The use of these transactions allowed Lehman Brothers to hide the true extent of its liabilities and make its financial position appear much stronger than it actually was.

As Lehman Brothers continued to engage in these transactions, the firm became increasingly leveraged and its risk exposure grew larger. In 2008, the housing market began to collapse, and Lehman Brothers' highly leveraged position made it vulnerable to significant losses. Despite warnings from analysts and investors, Lehman Brothers failed to take sufficient action to reduce its exposure to risky assets and continued to engage in risky financial transactions.

In September 2008, Lehman Brothers filed for bankruptcy, which triggered a global financial crisis and caused significant losses for investors and creditors. In the aftermath of the bankruptcy, investigations were launched into the accounting practices of Lehman Brothers, and it was revealed that the firm had engaged in extensive accounting fraud to conceal its true financial position.

- Early 2000s: Lehman Brothers begins engaging in a practice known as "repo 105," a type of short-term financing transaction that allows the firm to temporarily remove assets from its balance sheet to reduce its reported leverage ratio.
- 2004-2007: Lehman Brothers significantly increases its use of repo 105 transactions, enabling the firm to temporarily reduce its leverage ratio by as much as 10%.
- 2007: The U.S. housing market begins to collapse, leading to significant losses for Lehman Brothers.
- 2008: In March, a report by analysts raises concerns about Lehman Brothers' use of repo 105 transactions. In June, a whistleblower raises similar concerns to senior management, but no action is taken. In September, Lehman Brothers files for bankruptcy, triggering a global financial crisis.
- September 15, 2008: Lehman Brothers files for Chapter 11 bankruptcy, the largest bankruptcy filing in U.S. history at the time.
- September 17, 2008: It is revealed that Lehman Brothers had engaged in extensive accounting fraud, including the use of repo 105 transactions to conceal the true extent of its liabilities.
- October 2009: A report by the court-appointed examiner Anton Valukas reveals that Lehman Brothers had engaged in extensive accounting fraud, including the use of repo 105 transactions and the inflation of the

value of its real estate holdings.

- September 2010: The Securities and Exchange Commission (SEC) issues a report finding that Lehman Brothers violated securities laws by using deceptive accounting practices to mislead investors.
- 2011: The bankruptcy of Lehman Brothers is still ongoing, with the liquidation of its assets and liabilities taking several years.

The accounting fraud at Lehman Brothers was extensive and involved a range of illegal activities. The firm had used repo 105 transactions to conceal its true financial position, and it had also engaged in other fraudulent activities, such as inflating the value of its real estate holdings and misleading investors about the risks associated with its investments.

The collapse of Lehman Brothers in September 2008 had far-reaching implications for the global economy and financial system. The bankruptcy of the firm triggered a massive sell-off in financial markets, leading to significant losses for investors and creditors. The collapse of Lehman Brothers also led to a credit crunch, as banks became increasingly reluctant to lend money to each other, exacerbating the financial crisis.

One of the main impacts of the Lehman Brothers collapse was the onset of the global financial crisis, which had a significant impact on the global economy. The financial crisis led to a deep recession in many countries, as businesses and consumers faced significant financial difficulties. The global economy experienced a contraction in output, leading to job losses, reduced investment, and lower consumer spending.

The collapse of Lehman Brothers also had significant implications for the financial sector. The failure of a major financial institution like Lehman Brothers highlighted the risks and vulnerabilities of the financial system and raised concerns about the safety and stability of the sector. In the aftermath of the Lehman Brothers collapse, there was a significant increase in regulatory oversight and efforts to strengthen the financial system.

The collapse of Lehman Brothers also had political implications, as governments around the world were forced to intervene in the financial sector to prevent further collapses and stabilize the markets. Many countries implemented stimulus packages to support the economy and prevent a deeper recession.

The collapse of Lehman Brothers also led to significant changes in the financial industry, including changes in corporate governance, risk management practices, and the regulatory environment. The scandal exposed the dangers of unchecked greed and risky financial practices and prompted significant reforms to strengthen the integrity and stability of the financial sector.

In conclusion, the collapse of Lehman Brothers had significant and far-reaching implications for the global economy and financial system. The failure of the firm triggered a global financial crisis, led to significant losses for investors and creditors, and exposed the weaknesses and vulnerabilities of the financial sector. The scandal also led to significant regulatory reforms and changes in the financial industry to prevent future collapses and ensure the stability of the sector.

PARMALAT SCANDAL (2003)

The Parmalat Scandal was a financial scandal that occurred in Italy in 2003, involving the Italian dairy and food corporation Parmalat. The scandal was one of the largest financial frauds in European history and had a significant impact on the Italian economy and financial system.

The scandal began to unravel in December 2003 when Parmalat announced that a bank account containing €3.95 billion ($5 billion) did not exist, despite being listed on the company's balance sheet. It was later revealed that the company had used a series of fraudulent transactions and accounting techniques to hide its financial troubles, including the creation of offshore subsidiaries, fictitious transactions, and the fabrication of bank statements and other financial documents.

One of the key players in the scandal was Parmalat's founder and CEO, Calisto Tanzi, who was later convicted of fraud and sentenced to ten years in prison. Tanzi and other senior executives at the company had allegedly orchestrated the fraud, using the fictitious transactions and accounting techniques to artificially inflate the company's revenues and hide its mounting debts.

1. 1961: Parmalat is founded by Calisto Tanzi, who becomes the company's CEO.
2. 1990s: Parmalat begins expanding globally, acquiring subsidiaries and companies in Europe, South America, and elsewhere.

3. 2002: Parmalat's troubles begin to emerge, with the company reporting losses and facing increasing financial pressure.
4. November 2003: Parmalat announces plans to issue a bond worth €300 million, which is oversubscribed by investors.
5. December 2003: Parmalat announces that a bank account containing €3.95 billion ($5 billion) does not exist, despite being listed on the company's balance sheet. The company is unable to repay the bond, and questions begin to emerge about its financial reporting and accounting practices.
6. December 19, 2003: Parmalat's auditor, Grant Thornton, refuses to sign off on the company's accounts, citing irregularities in its financial reporting.
7. December 23, 2003: Parmalat files for bankruptcy protection in Italy, with debts estimated at €14 billion ($18 billion).
8. January 2004: Italian authorities launch an investigation into Parmalat and its executives, including Calisto Tanzi.
9. February 2004: Parmalat's chief financial officer, Fausto Tonna, is arrested on charges of fraud and insider trading.
10. April 2004: Parmalat's auditors, Deloitte, are fined €25 million by Italian regulators for their role in the scandal.
11. June 2004: Parmalat's banks, including Bank of America and Citigroup, are sued by the company's bondholders for their role in the fraud.
12. September 2004: Parmalat's former CFO, Fausto Tonna, is released from prison after striking a plea deal with prosecutors.
13. December 2004: Parmalat's former CEO, Calisto Tanzi, is arrested and charged with fraud and other crimes.
14. June 2005: Parmalat reaches a settlement with some of its creditors, including Deutsche Bank and Credit Suisse,

to pay back a portion of its debts.

15. December 2008: Calisto Tanzi is sentenced to ten years in prison for his role in the fraud.
16. January 2009: Parmalat reaches a settlement with Bank of America, Citigroup, and other banks involved in the scandal, recovering approximately €1.7 billion ($2.2 billion) in damages.
17. May 2013: Calisto Tanzi is released from prison after serving five years of his ten-year sentence.

The Parmalat Scandal had significant implications for the Italian economy and financial system. The scandal exposed weaknesses in the regulatory framework and corporate governance practices in Italy, leading to calls for reform and increased oversight. The Italian government was forced to intervene to prevent the collapse of Parmalat and its subsidiaries, which were major employers in the country. The scandal also had a significant impact on the Italian stock market, with the benchmark FTSE MIB index falling by 2.2% on the day that the fraud was announced.

The Parmalat Scandal also had wider implications for the global financial system, highlighting the risks and vulnerabilities of the corporate sector and the importance of transparency and accountability in financial reporting. The scandal led to increased scrutiny of financial reporting practices and accounting standards, particularly in the area of off-balance sheet financing and other forms of financial engineering.

In response to the scandal, Italy implemented a series of regulatory reforms to improve corporate governance and oversight, including the creation of a new regulatory authority to oversee financial reporting and accounting standards. The scandal also led to increased cooperation between regulators and law enforcement agencies across Europe and the United States, as they worked to investigate and prosecute those involved in the fraud.

In conclusion, the Parmalat Scandal was one of the largest financial frauds in European history and had significant implications for the Italian economy and financial system. The scandal exposed weaknesses in the regulatory framework and corporate governance practices in Italy and led to calls for reform and increased oversight. The Parmalat Scandal also had wider implications for the global financial system, highlighting the importance of transparency and accountability in financial reporting and leading to increased scrutiny of accounting standards and financial engineering practices.

SOCIÉTÉ GÉNÉRALE TRADING LOSSES (2008)

The Société Générale Trading Losses, also known as the Jerome Kerviel Affair, was a financial scandal that rocked one of France's largest banks in 2008. The scandal involved massive losses resulting from unauthorized trading activities by a single trader, Jerome Kerviel, which ultimately cost the bank billions of euros.

In late 2007 and early 2008, Jerome Kerviel, a junior trader at Société Générale, made a series of unauthorized trades on European equity index futures that ultimately led to losses of €4.9 billion ($6.7 billion) for the bank. Kerviel had been taking increasingly risky positions on behalf of the bank without proper authorization or oversight, using a combination of deception and technology to bypass risk management controls.

Kerviel had been working in the bank's Delta One division, which focuses on hedging strategies and risk management. He began making unauthorized trades in late 2006, and continued to do so throughout 2007. By the end of the year, he had taken positions worth €50 billion ($68 billion), which far exceeded the division's risk limits.

Kerviel used a combination of fake trades and forged documents to conceal his activities, and also employed sophisticated computer programs to manipulate risk management systems and bypass controls. He was able to hide his losses for months by offsetting them with fake trades and creating fictitious hedges.

When the trades were discovered in January 2008, Société Générale was forced to engage in a massive emergency stock sale to raise capital and offset the losses. The scandal caused significant damage to the bank's reputation and led to calls for increased regulation and oversight of the financial sector.

Following the discovery of the scandal, Société Générale launched an internal investigation and discovered that Kerviel had been able to evade risk management controls by creating fake hedges and altering computer codes. The bank's management team was criticized for failing to detect and prevent Kerviel's activities, and for not implementing sufficient controls and oversight to prevent similar incidents in the future.

1. Late 2006: Junior trader Jerome Kerviel begins making unauthorized trades on European equity index futures in Société Générale's Delta One division.

2. 2007: Kerviel continues to make unauthorized trades, taking positions worth €50 billion ($68 billion), far exceeding the division's risk limits.

3. January 18, 2008: Société Générale discovers the unauthorized trades and launches an investigation.

4. January 24, 2008: Société Générale announces that Kerviel's unauthorized trades have resulted in losses of €4.9 billion ($6.7 billion).

5. January 28, 2008: Société Générale's CEO Daniel Bouton resigns.

6. February 8, 2008: Société Générale announces that it will conduct a €5.5 billion ($7.5 billion) capital increase to offset the losses.

7. February 21, 2008: Jerome Kerviel is arrested and charged with forgery, breach of trust, and unauthorized computer use.

8. March 18, 2008: Société Générale releases the findings of its internal investigation, which reveals that Kerviel used a combination of fake trades, forged

documents, and computer programs to manipulate risk management systems and bypass controls.

9. May 12, 2010: Kerviel is found guilty of all charges and sentenced to three years in prison.

10. October 24, 2012: Société Générale is fined €4 million by the French Financial Markets Authority for failing to implement adequate risk management controls.

11. November 23, 2016: An appeals court in France upholds Kerviel's conviction, but reduces his sentence to two years and orders him to pay back €1 million ($1.1 million) in damages.

Kerviel was ultimately convicted of forgery, breach of trust, and unauthorized computer use, and sentenced to three years in prison. However, the scandal had wider implications for the banking industry as a whole, highlighting the risks associated with unchecked trading activity and the need for greater transparency and accountability in the financial sector.

The Société Générale trading losses had significant consequences for unchecked trading activity and led to a number of new controls being implemented in the financial industry.

Firstly, the scandal highlighted the importance of strengthening risk management controls and improving the supervision of trading activities. Banks and financial institutions began to implement tighter controls on trading activities, including stricter risk management processes, more robust internal controls, and greater transparency in financial reporting.

Secondly, the scandal also prompted greater scrutiny of the role of financial regulators in preventing trading fraud and ensuring financial stability. Regulators worldwide began to take a more active role in monitoring and supervising trading activities, including implementing stricter rules around the reporting of trading positions and the use of complex financial instruments.

Thirdly, the Société Générale scandal also contributed to a wider shift in the financial industry towards a more ethical and responsible approach to business. This included a greater focus on corporate social responsibility, greater emphasis on employee training and compliance programs, and more effective whistle-blower protection and reporting mechanisms.

In addition, the scandal had significant financial consequences for Société Générale, with the bank forced to write off nearly $7 billion in losses and undertake a €5.5 billion capital increase to offset the damage. The scandal also led to the resignation of the bank's CEO and significant reputational damage to the institution.

Overall, the Société Générale trading losses had a significant impact on the financial industry, leading to a renewed focus on risk management, regulatory oversight, and ethical behavior. It represented a cautionary tale of the risks associated with unchecked trading activity and the importance of maintaining strict controls and compliance measures in the financial sector.

MF GLOBAL SCANDAL (2011)

The MF Global scandal was a financial scandal that rocked the global financial industry in 2011, when the futures and commodities brokerage firm MF Global filed for bankruptcy following a series of disastrous investments in European sovereign debt. The scandal involved a complex web of financial transactions and fraud that ultimately led to the loss of billions of dollars of customer funds, and the resignation of CEO Jon Corzine.

The origins of the MF Global scandal can be traced back to the company's decision to invest heavily in European sovereign debt, particularly bonds issued by troubled countries such as Italy, Spain, and Portugal. Despite warnings from regulators and analysts, MF Global continued to invest heavily in these bonds, leveraging its positions to boost its profits.

The technical details leading to the MF Global scandal were complex and involved a number of different financial instruments and strategies. At the heart of the scandal was MF Global's decision to invest heavily in European sovereign debt, particularly bonds issued by Italy, Spain, and Portugal.

To finance these investments, MF Global used a variety of financial instruments, including repurchase agreements (repos) and credit default swaps (CDS). In a typical repo transaction, MF Global would borrow funds from a counterparty, using its European sovereign debt as collateral. If the value of the collateral fell below a certain level, the counterparty would be entitled to a margin call, requiring MF Global to provide additional collateral or cash to cover the shortfall.

Similarly, in a CDS transaction, MF Global would buy protection against the default of a particular bond or group of bonds. If a default occurred, the protection would pay out, providing a source of liquidity for MF Global.

However, when the European sovereign debt crisis worsened in late 2011, the value of MF Global's European sovereign debt holdings began to decline rapidly, triggering margin calls and forcing the company to provide additional collateral or cash. In an effort to cover these shortfalls, MF Global began transferring customer funds to cover its own positions, in violation of securities laws and a breach of customer trust.

However, when the European sovereign debt crisis worsened in late 2011, MF Global's investments quickly turned sour, with the value of the bonds plummeting and triggering a margin call on the company's trading accounts. In an effort to cover the losses and avoid bankruptcy, MF Global began transferring customer funds to cover its own shortfalls, a violation of securities laws and a breach of customer trust.

The transfer of customer funds ultimately led to the bankruptcy of MF Global, and the loss of more than $1 billion in customer funds. The scandal also sparked a major investigation by the U.S. Department of Justice and the Securities and Exchange Commission, leading to multiple civil and criminal charges against MF Global executives, including CEO Jon Corzine.

The scandal had significant consequences for the global financial industry, leading to a renewed focus on regulatory oversight and the protection of customer funds. It also highlighted the risks associated with complex financial transactions and the need for greater transparency and accountability in the financial industry.

The MF Global scandal had significant impacts on the financial industry and the broader economy. Here are some of the key impacts:

1. Loss of customer funds: The scandal resulted in the loss of more than $1 billion in customer funds, which had a devastating impact on the affected customers. Many customers were small farmers and traders who relied on MF Global to manage their money and were left with no way to recover their losses.

2. Trust in the financial industry: The scandal eroded trust in the financial industry, particularly among retail investors who were already skeptical of the industry after the 2008 financial crisis. The fact that customer funds were misused in this way further undermined confidence in the financial system.

3. Regulatory changes: In the wake of the MF Global scandal, regulators implemented a number of new rules and regulations aimed at preventing a similar incident from occurring in the future. These included stricter capital requirements, increased transparency, and improved customer protection measures.

4. Legal repercussions: MF Global's bankruptcy and the subsequent investigation led to a number of lawsuits and legal actions against the company and its executives. While some settlements were reached, many customers and investors were left without adequate compensation for their losses.

5. Impact on commodity markets: MF Global was a major player in commodity markets, and its collapse had significant impacts on these markets. The company's liquidation led to a temporary disruption of markets, as investors struggled to fill the void left by MF Global's departure.

Overall, the MF Global scandal represented a cautionary tale of the risks associated with unchecked risk-taking in the financial industry, and the importance of maintaining strict controls and compliance measures to protect investors and ensure financial stability.

PEREGRINE FINANCIAL GROUP FRAUD (2012)

The Peregrine Financial Group, also known as PFG, was a futures brokerage firm based in Cedar Falls, Iowa, that collapsed in July 2012 following the revelation of a massive fraud. The company had been in business for more than 20 years and had been regarded as one of the most reputable futures brokerages in the industry.

In July 2012, the founder and CEO of PFG, Russell Wasendorf Sr., attempted suicide in his car outside the company's headquarters. Shortly thereafter, it was discovered that Wasendorf had been embezzling millions of dollars from the company over a period of several years. Wasendorf had forged bank statements and other financial documents to conceal his theft, which ultimately amounted to around $215 million in customer funds.

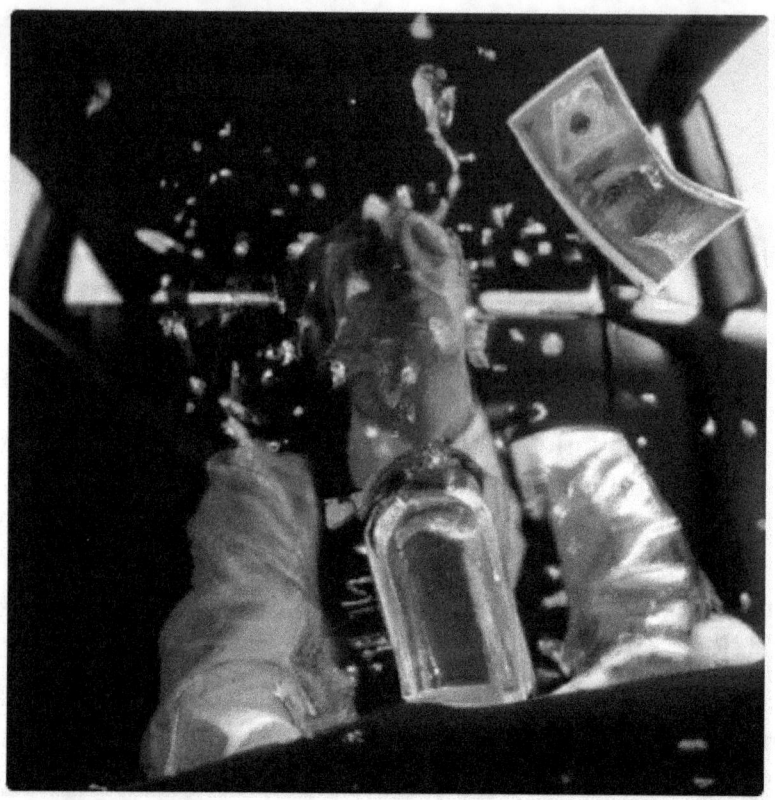

The fraud at PFG had a number of significant consequences, both for the company itself and for the broader financial industry. Some of the key impacts included:

Customer losses: The most immediate impact of the PFG fraud was the loss of customer funds. Many customers were left with little or no recourse to recover their losses, and some have still not been fully compensated.

Industry trust: The PFG fraud eroded trust in the futures industry, particularly among retail investors who were already skeptical of the industry following previous scandals such as the MF Global collapse.

Regulatory changes: In response to the PFG fraud, regulators implemented a number of new rules and regulations aimed at preventing similar incidents from occurring in the future.

These included increased oversight and more stringent capital requirements for futures brokerages.

Legal repercussions: The PFG fraud resulted in a number of lawsuits and legal actions against the company and its executives. Wasendorf ultimately pleaded guilty to multiple charges of fraud and was sentenced to 50 years in prison.

Impact on the futures industry: The collapse of PFG had significant impacts on the futures industry, particularly in the United States where it was one of the largest futures brokerages. The company's bankruptcy and subsequent liquidation led to a temporary disruption of markets, as investors struggled to fill the void left by PFG's departure.

1. 1980s: Russell Wasendorf Sr. founds Peregrine Financial Group, a futures brokerage firm based in Cedar Falls, Iowa.
2. Early 2000s: Peregrine Financial Group expands rapidly, becoming one of the largest futures brokerages in the United States.
3. 2008: The financial crisis hits, causing a decline in business for Peregrine Financial Group and other financial institutions.
4. 2010: The Commodity Futures Trading Commission (CFTC) begins investigating Peregrine Financial Group for potential violations of customer fund segregation rules.
5. 2012: In February, Peregrine Financial Group reports a capital shortfall to the CFTC and begins seeking additional financing to cover the shortfall.
6. July 9, 2012: Russell Wasendorf Sr. attempts suicide outside Peregrine Financial Group's headquarters.
7. July 10, 2012: It is discovered that Wasendorf had been embezzling customer funds for years, totaling around $215 million.
8. July 10, 2012: Peregrine Financial Group files for bankruptcy and is later liquidated.

9. July 13, 2012: The CFTC files a lawsuit against Peregrine Financial Group, alleging violations of customer fund segregation rules.
10. July 23, 2012: Wasendorf is arrested and charged with multiple counts of fraud.
11. September 2012: Wasendorf pleads guilty to multiple charges of fraud.
12. January 2013: Wasendorf is sentenced to 50 years in prison for his role in the Peregrine Financial Group fraud.

Overall, the PFG fraud highlighted the need for greater transparency and oversight in the financial industry, particularly in the futures markets. While regulatory changes have been implemented in response to the fraud, the impact on affected customers and investors cannot be underestimated, and many are still struggling to recover their losses.

NORTHERN ROCK CRISIS (2007)

The Northern Rock Crisis was a banking crisis that occurred in the United Kingdom in 2007. It was triggered by the global financial crisis and led to the first run on a British bank in over 150 years. The crisis had far-reaching implications for the UK economy and the financial sector as a whole.

Northern Rock was a mortgage lender that relied heavily on borrowing from the wholesale money markets to finance its lending activities. When the global financial crisis hit in 2007, the cost of borrowing on these markets increased sharply, making it more difficult for Northern Rock to raise the funds it needed to continue operating.

In September 2007, the Bank of England provided emergency funding to Northern Rock to prevent it from going bankrupt. However, news of the bank's financial troubles quickly spread and caused a panic among depositors, leading to a run on the bank. Customers queued outside Northern Rock branches to withdraw their savings, leading to scenes of chaos and panic on the streets.

1. In 2007, the global financial crisis began to take hold, causing disruptions in the financial markets and making it more difficult for banks to access funding.
2. Northern Rock, a UK-based mortgage lender, relied heavily on borrowing from the wholesale money markets to finance its lending activities.
3. In September 2007, the cost of borrowing on the

        wholesale markets increased sharply, making it more difficult for Northern Rock to raise the funds it needed to continue operating.

4. On September 13, 2007, the Bank of England provided emergency funding to Northern Rock in an effort to prevent the bank from going bankrupt.
5. News of Northern Rock's financial troubles quickly spread, causing a panic among depositors.
6. From September 14, 2007, customers began queuing outside Northern Rock branches to withdraw their savings, leading to scenes of chaos and panic on the streets.
7. On September 17, 2007, the UK government issued a statement guaranteeing all deposits held by Northern Rock customers.
8. The Bank of England continued to provide emergency funding to Northern Rock, but the bank's financial position continued to deteriorate.
9. In February 2008, the UK government announced that it would nationalize Northern Rock in an effort to prevent the bank from collapsing and to protect depositors.
10. The nationalization of Northern Rock was controversial and raised concerns about the stability of the UK financial sector.

The UK government eventually stepped in to nationalize Northern Rock in February 2008, in an effort to prevent the bank from collapsing and to protect depositors. The nationalization was controversial and raised concerns about the stability of the UK financial sector.

The Northern Rock Crisis had significant economic and political consequences. It contributed to a wider loss of confidence in the UK banking system and led to increased regulation and scrutiny of the financial sector. It also highlighted the need for better risk management and more robust regulatory oversight of financial institutions.

The crisis also had implications for the broader UK economy. It contributed to a slowdown in economic growth and led to increased government borrowing to fund the bank bailout. It also contributed to a wider crisis of confidence in the global financial system, which had far-reaching consequences for economies around the world.

In conclusion, the Northern Rock Crisis was a significant event in the history of the UK financial sector. It highlighted the need for better risk management and regulatory oversight of financial institutions, and had far-reaching consequences for the UK economy and the global financial system.

AIG FINANCIAL PRODUCTS SCANDAL (2008)

AIG Financial Products was a subsidiary of the American International Group (AIG) that provided credit default swaps (CDS) and other financial derivatives. These CDS were insurance policies that paid out in the event of a default on a particular asset, such as a mortgage-backed security. During the housing bubble of the mid-2000s, AIG Financial Products became heavily involved in insuring mortgage-backed securities and other risky assets, including collateralized debt obligations (CDOs).

When the housing market collapsed in 2007 and defaults on these assets began to mount, AIG Financial Products found itself on the hook for billions of dollars in insurance payouts. However, the company did not have the reserves to cover these losses and was in danger of collapsing. To avoid this, the U.S. government stepped in with a bailout package worth $85 billion in September 2008.

The AIG Financial Products scandal was not just a case of a company making risky bets and losing. It was also a case of fraudulent accounting and misleading investors. The company used a number of accounting tricks to hide the true extent of its losses and the risks it was taking on. For example, AIG Financial Products used mark-to-model accounting, which allowed it to value its assets based on its own models rather than market prices. This meant that it could overvalue its assets and understate its liabilities.

AIG Financial Products also used a practice known as regulatory capital arbitrage, in which it moved assets off its balance sheet to avoid regulatory requirements for capital reserves. This made the company appear to be better capitalized than it actually was, which in turn made it easier to obtain credit.

These are the major events that led to the AIG Financial Products scandal, which had far-reaching implications for the financial industry and the wider economy.

1. 1987: American International Group (AIG) creates the Financial Products division (AIGFP) as a way to offer insurance contracts to investors, which would allow them to transfer the risk of their investments to AIG.

2. 2000: AIGFP begins to sell credit default swaps (CDS) which are contracts that insure against the default of corporate bonds.

3. 2005: The Securities and Exchange Commission (SEC) and the Department of Justice (DOJ) begin investigations into AIG's accounting practices, including transactions with General Re Corporation that were used to inflate AIG's reserves.

4. 2006: AIG's CEO Maurice "Hank" Greenberg resigns amidst allegations of accounting fraud. He is replaced by Martin J. Sullivan.

5. March 2008: AIG reports a $7.8 billion loss in the fourth quarter of 2007 due to the subprime mortgage crisis.

6. September 2008: Lehman Brothers files for bankruptcy, triggering a financial crisis. AIG's stock begins to decline rapidly, and the company is unable to obtain short-term funding to cover its obligations.

7. September 16, 2008: The Federal Reserve Bank of New York approves an $85 billion loan to AIG in exchange for an 80% stake in the company. The loan is later increased to $182 billion.

8. October 2008: The House Oversight and Government

Reform Committee holds a hearing on AIG's collapse and its use of credit default swaps. AIGFP executives testify that the company had sold CDS without fully understanding the risks involved.

9. February 2009: AIG reports a $61.7 billion loss for the fourth quarter of 2008, the largest quarterly loss in US corporate history.

10. March 2009: AIG announces plans to pay $165 million in retention bonuses to AIGFP executives, sparking public outrage.

11. April 2009: AIG releases a list of banks that received payments from the company using the government bailout funds. The list includes Goldman Sachs, Deutsche Bank, and Société Générale, among others.

12. March 2010: The Financial Crisis Inquiry Commission releases its report on the causes of the financial crisis. The report highlights AIG's use of credit default swaps as a major contributing factor to the crisis.

13. January 2013: AIG repays the government bailout funds and exits government ownership.

Another issue with AIG Financial Products was the lack of oversight and risk management. The company was operating largely outside of AIG's traditional insurance business and was subject to much less regulatory scrutiny. As a result, it was able to take on huge risks without proper controls in place to manage those risks.

The fallout from the AIG Financial Products scandal was significant. The company was forced to pay out billions in insurance claims and was bailed out by the U.S. government to prevent its collapse. The scandal also had wider implications for the financial system as a whole. The collapse of AIG Financial Products contributed to the freezing of credit markets and the global financial crisis of 2008.

The AIG scandal had significant implications for the global economy. AIG's collapse could have led to the failure of several major financial institutions and caused a complete collapse of the financial system, similar to the Great Depression of the 1930s. The US government's rescue of AIG had a massive impact on the national debt, and the government had to provide extensive financial support to prevent the collapse of the financial system.

The bailout also raised questions about the role of government in the economy and the extent to which it should intervene in private enterprise. Critics argued that the government's intervention in the economy was an overreach of its power and that it set a dangerous precedent for future government interventions.

The AIG scandal also highlighted the risks associated with the unregulated and complex financial instruments, such as credit default swaps, which played a significant role in AIG's collapse. It led to a re-evaluation of the regulatory framework for financial markets and instruments, with many calling for stricter regulation and oversight to prevent future financial crises.

Furthermore, the AIG scandal had global repercussions, as the company had significant operations and influence in financial markets worldwide. The fallout from the scandal led to increased scrutiny of financial institutions and markets around the world, as investors and regulators became more aware of the risks associated with complex financial instruments and the potential for widespread financial contagion.

Overall, the AIG scandal had far-reaching implications for the global economy, leading to a re-evaluation of the role of government in the economy, increased regulation and oversight of financial markets, and a renewed focus on the potential risks associated with complex financial instruments.

In response to the scandal, regulators and policymakers introduced a number of reforms to increase oversight of the financial system and reduce the risk of similar scandals occurring in the future. These reforms included the Dodd-Frank Act, which introduced new regulations for derivatives trading and established the Consumer Financial Protection Bureau.

OLYMPUS ACCOUNTING SCANDAL (2011)

The Olympus accounting scandal, also known as the Olympus scandal or Olympusgate, was a major corporate scandal that unfolded in 2011, involving the Japanese multinational corporation, Olympus Corporation. The scandal involved a massive accounting fraud, which was perpetrated over a period of two decades, and involved senior executives at the company.

The scandal began to unravel in October 2011, when Michael Woodford, the CEO of Olympus, was fired after raising concerns about irregular payments made by the company. Woodford alleged that the payments were part of a scheme to hide losses that the company had incurred from speculative investments in the late 1980s and early 1990s.

After Woodford's dismissal, he publicly accused the company of engaging in a cover-up and fraud, and he approached the authorities in Japan and the UK with his concerns. Following an investigation, it was revealed that Olympus had used fraudulent accounting practices, including hiding losses through inflated payments to advisors, overpaying for acquisitions, and falsifying financial statements.

The extent of the fraud was significant, with the company revealing that it had hidden losses of approximately $1.7 billion over a period of two decades. The fraud had been orchestrated by senior executives at the company, including the former chairman and CEO, as well as several board members and auditors.

The scandal had major implications for Olympus, with its share price plummeting and its reputation severely damaged. The company faced multiple lawsuits from shareholders and was investigated by regulators in Japan, the US, and Europe. Several executives at the company were arrested and prosecuted, including the former chairman and CEO, who was sentenced to ten years in prison.

The scandal also had wider implications for corporate governance and the accounting profession in Japan. The scandal exposed weaknesses in the regulatory framework and accounting standards in Japan, and led to calls for reform and increased transparency. It also highlighted the importance of whistleblower protection and the need for a culture of transparency and accountability in corporate governance.

1. In the 1980s, Olympus began acquiring companies in the medical equipment and imaging industries, including Gyrus Group PLC in 2008.
2. In October 2011, Olympus CEO Michael Woodford was fired after questioning suspicious payments related to acquisitions.
3. Woodford then brought his concerns to the attention of the media and regulators, alleging that the company had been involved in a $1.7 billion accounting fraud scheme to cover up investment losses dating back to the 1990s.
4. The scandal led to an investigation by Japanese authorities and the arrest of several Olympus executives.
5. In December 2011, Olympus issued a report admitting to hiding investment losses for decades and covering up the fraud with inflated fees paid to advisers.
6. The scandal resulted in a significant drop in Olympus' stock price and financial losses for the company.
7. The company was also fined by regulators in Japan and

the United States for violating securities laws.

8. The scandal led to significant changes in corporate governance in Japan, as well as increased scrutiny of accounting practices and whistleblower protection laws.

Overall, the Olympus accounting scandal was a significant event in the corporate world, exposing the risks of fraudulent accounting practices and the importance of strong corporate governance and regulatory oversight. The scandal had lasting consequences for Olympus, its shareholders, and the accounting profession in Japan.

ALLIED IRISH BANK HIDDEN LOANS SCANDAL (2009)

The Allied Irish Bank Hidden Loans Scandal of 2009 involved allegations of wrongdoing and unethical behavior at one of Ireland's largest banks, Allied Irish Bank (AIB).

The scandal began in 2008 when it was revealed that a number of senior executives at AIB had been involved in a scheme to conceal large loans from the bank's balance sheet. The loans were given to a group of ten high-profile Irish businessmen, including Sean Fitzpatrick, the bank's former chairman.

The loans were made through an offshore subsidiary of the bank, and were not reported on the bank's financial statements. It was alleged that the loans were used to purchase shares in the bank, thereby artificially inflating its stock price.

As the scandal unfolded, it became clear that the bank's top executives had been aware of the loans, but had failed to disclose them to regulators or shareholders. The Irish government was forced to intervene, injecting €3.5 billion in taxpayer funds to stabilize the bank and prevent a collapse.

The fallout from the scandal was significant, with several top executives at AIB resigning or being forced out of their positions. The bank was also fined €2 million by the Central Bank of Ireland for breaching regulatory requirements.

The Allied Irish Bank Hidden Loans Scandal had a significant impact on the Irish economy, which was already facing a severe financial crisis at the time. The revelation of the hidden loans further eroded public trust in the country's banking system and led to increased scrutiny of the government's role in regulating and overseeing the banks.

1. In 2008, Allied Irish Bank (AIB) suffered significant losses due to the global financial crisis and the collapse of the Irish property market.
2. In November 2008, AIB disclosed that it had extended loans to ten of its executives, including its CEO, totaling €87 million.
3. AIB initially claimed that the loans were approved by its board of directors and were in compliance with all regulations.
4. However, it was soon revealed that the loans had been granted without proper disclosure or approval, and that the bank's internal controls had been inadequate.
5. In December 2008, the Irish government injected €3.5 billion into AIB to shore up its capital base.
6. In January 2009, the Financial Regulator launched an investigation into the hidden loans, and AIB's CEO resigned.
7. In March 2009, AIB's Chairman, Dermot Gleeson, also resigned, and the Irish government announced that it would take a 25% stake in the bank in exchange for additional capital.
8. The investigation by the Financial Regulator revealed that the loans were part of a broader pattern of irregular lending practices at AIB.
9. In 2010, AIB reported a record loss of €12 billion, largely due to bad loans in the Irish property market.
10. In 2011, the Irish government was forced to nationalize AIB as part of a broader effort to stabilize the Irish banking system in the wake of the financial crisis.

11. The AIB scandal contributed to a loss of public trust in the Irish banking sector and had wider implications for the Irish economy, which was plunged into recession in the aftermath of the financial crisis.

The scandal exposed a lack of oversight and accountability within the banking sector and highlighted the need for greater transparency and regulation. The Irish government was forced to intervene to stabilize the banking system and prevent a complete collapse. This resulted in a costly bailout that had long-lasting effects on the country's economy and society.

The bailout of Allied Irish Bank and other troubled banks contributed to a ballooning of Ireland's national debt, which reached unsustainable levels. The government was forced to implement austerity measures, including significant spending cuts and tax hikes, in an effort to balance the budget and reduce the debt burden.

The fallout from the scandal also led to changes in the Irish banking system. The government established a new regulatory body, the Central Bank of Ireland, with increased powers to oversee and regulate the banking sector. The Irish banking system also underwent significant restructuring, with many of the smaller banks being merged or acquired by larger institutions.

The Allied Irish Bank Hidden Loans Scandal serves as a cautionary tale about the dangers of unchecked greed and corruption within the financial sector. It underscores the need for strong regulation, oversight, and accountability to prevent such abuses from occurring in the future.

ANGLO IRISH BANK SCANDAL (2009)

The Anglo Irish Bank Scandal of 2009 is regarded as one of the most significant financial crises in the history of Ireland. The crisis was a result of the collapse of Anglo Irish Bank, which was one of the country's largest banks at the time. The collapse of the bank had far-reaching consequences, leading to a significant downturn in the Irish economy and a series of subsequent bailouts by the government.

The roots of the crisis can be traced back to the early 2000s when Anglo Irish Bank, under the leadership of CEO Sean FitzPatrick, began engaging in high-risk lending practices, particularly in the area of property development. The bank aggressively expanded its lending to property developers, who used the money to fuel a massive property bubble in Ireland.

The bank's lending practices were reckless, with the bank lending billions of euros to developers without conducting proper due diligence or assessing the risks involved. The bank also engaged in a practice known as "window dressing," where it manipulated its accounts to give the impression of financial stability.

The bank's risky lending practices eventually caught up with it in 2008 when the Irish property market crashed, leaving many developers unable to repay their loans. This led to a surge in bad debts, causing the bank's share price to plummet. In September 2008, the Irish government was forced to intervene and nationalize the bank in an effort to prevent its collapse.

The nationalization of Anglo Irish Bank had significant implications for the Irish economy, as it left the government with a massive bill to cover the bank's losses. The government was forced to provide billions of euros in bailout funds to keep the bank afloat, leading to a significant increase in national debt.

In addition to the financial impact of the crisis, the Anglo Irish Bank Scandal also had a significant political fallout. The scandal highlighted the cozy relationship between the banking sector and the Irish government, with many politicians accused of turning a blind eye to the bank's risky lending practices. The crisis also led to a loss of confidence in the Irish banking system and resulted in a series of regulatory reforms aimed at preventing similar crises from occurring in the future.

In the aftermath of the crisis, several key figures associated with the bank were implicated in a number of legal investigations. Sean FitzPatrick, the former CEO of Anglo Irish Bank, was charged with multiple counts of fraud and was sentenced to three years in prison in 2016. Other senior executives of the bank were also charged with a range of offenses, including fraud, forgery, and false accounting.

1. Early 2000s: Anglo Irish Bank begins engaging in high-risk lending practices, particularly in the area of property development.
2. 2005-2007: The bank aggressively expands its lending to property developers, who use the money to fuel a massive property bubble in Ireland.
3. 2008: The Irish property market crashes, leaving many developers unable to repay their loans.
4. September 2008: The Irish government intervenes and nationalizes Anglo Irish Bank in an effort to prevent its collapse.
5. Late 2008: The government provides billions of euros in bailout funds to keep the bank afloat.
6. 2009: The Irish government announces a guarantee for all deposits in Irish banks, including Anglo Irish Bank.

7. 2010: An investigation by the Irish Financial Regulator reveals that Anglo Irish Bank engaged in a practice known as "window dressing," manipulating its accounts to give the impression of financial stability.
8. 2010-2011: The Irish government provides further bailout funds to Anglo Irish Bank.
9. 2011: The bank is liquidated, and its assets are transferred to a new entity, the Irish Bank Resolution Corporation (IBRC).
10. 2012: The Irish government announces that it will wind down IBRC, transferring its remaining assets to the National Asset Management Agency (NAMA).
11. 2013: The former CEO of Anglo Irish Bank, Sean FitzPatrick, is arrested and charged with multiple counts of fraud.
12. 2016: FitzPatrick is sentenced to three years in prison after being found guilty of multiple charges of fraud, forgery, and false accounting.
13. 2020: The Irish government announces a compensation scheme for victims of the scandal, including small business owners and homeowners who were affected by the collapse of the property market.

These events highlight the gradual deterioration of Anglo Irish Bank's financial position, as well as the government's increasing involvement in attempting to prevent its collapse. The fallout from the scandal has had significant economic, political, and social consequences for Ireland, leading to a loss of confidence in the Irish banking system and a series of regulatory reforms aimed at preventing similar crises from occurring in the future.

Overall, the Anglo Irish Bank Scandal of 2009 had far-reaching consequences for the Irish economy, politics, and society as a whole. The crisis highlighted the dangers of reckless lending practices and led to a significant overhaul of the Irish banking system.

COLONIAL BANK FRAUD SCANDAL (2009)

The Colonial Bank Fraud Scandal of 2009 was a financial scandal involving the Colonial Bank, which was one of the largest banks in the southeastern United States. The scandal involved fraudulent activity by the bank's senior executives and resulted in a significant financial loss for the bank's investors, as well as the Federal Deposit Insurance Corporation (FDIC), which ultimately had to pay out billions of dollars to cover the bank's losses.

The roots of the scandal can be traced back to 2002 when the Colonial Bank began engaging in high-risk lending practices, particularly in the area of real estate development. The bank aggressively expanded its lending to real estate developers, who used the money to fuel a massive real estate bubble in the southeastern United States.

The bank's lending practices were reckless, with the bank lending billions of dollars to developers without conducting proper due diligence or assessing the risks involved. The bank also engaged in a practice known as "double booking," where it recorded the same loans multiple times on its books to inflate its profits and assets.

The double booking scheme used by the Colonial Bank involved the creation of a complex network of sham companies, which were used to manipulate the bank's accounting records. The scheme worked as follows:

1. The Colonial Bank would make a loan to a real estate developer, recording the loan as an asset on its books.
2. The bank would then sell the loan to one of the sham companies, often at a discount, in exchange for a fee or commission. The bank would record the sale of the loan as revenue, even though the loan had not actually been repaid.
3. The sham company would then sell the same loan to another sham company, again at a discount, and the process would repeat itself several times.
4. Each time the loan was sold, the Colonial Bank would record the sale as revenue, even though the loan had not been repaid. This would inflate the bank's revenue and assets, making it appear more profitable and financially stable than it actually was.
5. In some cases, the sham companies would even create fake loan payments to further inflate the bank's profits.
6. To further conceal the fraudulent activity, the bank's executives would create false documents and accounting records to make it appear as though the sham companies were legitimate businesses with real assets and revenue.

Overall, the double booking scheme used by the Colonial Bank was a highly sophisticated and complex fraud, designed to deceive regulators, investors, and other stakeholders. The scheme allowed the bank to inflate its profits and assets, and to conceal the true extent of the activities.

The bank's risky lending practices eventually caught up with it in 2008 when the U.S. housing market crashed, leaving many developers unable to repay their loans. This led to a surge in bad debts, causing the bank's share price to plummet. In August 2009, the bank was seized by federal regulators and later declared bankrupt.

The fallout from the Colonial Bank Fraud Scandal had far-reaching consequences. The FDIC had to pay out over $2.8 billion to cover the bank's losses, making it one of the largest payouts in the history of the FDIC. The scandal also had a significant impact on the wider U.S. economy, contributing to the 2008 financial crisis and leading to a loss of confidence in the U.S. banking system.

The scandal also resulted in several key figures associated with the bank facing legal action. In 2011, Lee Farkas, the former chairman of Colonial Bank, was sentenced to 30 years in prison for his role in the fraud. Other senior executives of the bank were also charged with a range of offenses, including conspiracy, bank fraud, and money laundering.

Overall, the Colonial Bank Fraud Scandal of 2009 had far-reaching consequences for the U.S. economy and the banking sector. The scandal highlighted the dangers of reckless lending practices and the importance of proper regulation and oversight in the banking sector. It also led to a significant overhaul of the U.S. banking system and increased scrutiny of financial institutions in the aftermath of the financial crisis.

BERNIE MADOFF
PONZI SCHEME (2008)

The Bernie Madoff Ponzi Scheme was one of the largest financial frauds in history, with losses estimated at over $65 billion. The scheme, which operated for over two decades, involved the creation of a complex web of financial instruments and investment vehicles, which were used to deceive investors and conceal the fraudulent activity from regulators and law enforcement.

Bernard Madoff was a well-respected Wall Street financier who had been a prominent figure in the financial world for several decades. He had served as the chairman of the NASDAQ stock exchange and had established himself as a trusted investment advisor to many wealthy individuals and institutions.

Madoff's Ponzi scheme began in the 1980s and continued until 2008, when the scheme collapsed in the wake of the global financial crisis. The scheme involved Madoff's investment firm, Bernard L. Madoff Investment Securities LLC, which purported to generate high returns for investors by using a proprietary trading strategy known as the "split-strike conversion."

In reality, Madoff's investment strategy was a complete fiction. Rather than investing clients' money in the markets, Madoff simply deposited the money into a bank account and used it to pay off earlier investors, while also paying himself and his family members exorbitant fees.

Madoff's scheme was able to continue for so long because he

used a variety of techniques to deceive investors and regulators. He produced false account statements and other documents, and created a network of feeder funds that funneled money into his investment firm. He also used his reputation as a respected member of the financial community to convince investors to entrust him with their money.

Bernie Madoff's Ponzi scheme was a complex and sophisticated fraud that involved a number of technical steps. Some of the key steps in the scheme included:

1. Creating a false investment strategy: Madoff created a false investment strategy called the "split-strike conversion strategy," which he claimed involved investing in a basket of stocks and using options to limit risk. In reality, this strategy did not exist and Madoff was simply using new investors' money to pay off earlier investors.

2. Falsifying investment records: Madoff and his associates created false investment records to make it appear as if the investments were performing well. These records included falsified trade confirmations, account statements, and other documents that made it seem as if the investments were generating consistent returns.

3. Using feeder funds: Madoff used a network of feeder funds to attract investors to his Ponzi scheme. These funds were created by other investment firms and were used to invest in Madoff's fund. The feeder funds took a percentage of the investor's money as a fee, while Madoff took an additional fee for managing the investments.

4. Offering high returns: Madoff promised investors high returns, which he claimed were based on his proprietary investment strategy. These returns were often consistent and predictable, which helped to attract new investors and maintain the confidence of existing investors.

5. Discouraging withdrawals: Madoff discouraged

investors from withdrawing their money by imposing penalties and fees for early withdrawals. He also created the illusion of a waiting list for new investors, which made it seem as if demand for the investments was high and further reinforced the idea that the investments were safe and legitimate.

6. Keeping everything in-house: Madoff used his own accounting firm to manage the books and records for his investment fund. This allowed him to manipulate the records and conceal the true nature of the fraud from regulators and auditors.

Overall, Madoff's Ponzi scheme was a highly sophisticated and complex fraud that relied on a variety of technical steps to deceive investors and regulators. The scheme was able to continue for decades because Madoff was able to create the illusion of legitimacy and maintain the trust of his investors, despite the fact that the investments were completely fraudulent.

The collapse of Madoff's scheme in 2008 sent shockwaves through the financial world, as thousands of investors suddenly realized that they had lost billions of dollars. The scandal had far-reaching consequences, leading to a loss of confidence in the financial system and prompting calls for greater regulation and oversight of the investment industry.

In the aftermath of the scandal, Madoff was arrested and charged with numerous counts of securities fraud, wire fraud, and money laundering. He ultimately pleaded guilty to 11 felony charges and was sentenced to 150 years in prison, one of the longest sentences ever handed down in a financial fraud case.

The Bernie Madoff Ponzi Scheme remains a cautionary tale for investors and regulators alike, highlighting the dangers of investment fraud and the need for greater transparency and oversight in the financial industry. The scandal also had a significant impact on the victims of the fraud, many of whom lost their life savings and were left struggling to rebuild their finances in the wake of the collapse.

Some of the wider implications of the scandal include:

1. Loss of confidence in the financial system: The Madoff scandal contributed to a loss of confidence in the financial system, as investors realized that even well-respected figures in the industry could engage in fraud. This loss of confidence had ripple effects throughout the global financial system and helped to contribute to the severity of the global financial crisis.

2. Increased scrutiny of the financial industry: In the wake of the Madoff scandal, regulators and lawmakers around the world called for increased scrutiny of the financial industry. This led to the implementation of new regulations and oversight mechanisms, including the Dodd-Frank Act in the United States and the European Union's Markets in Financial Instruments Directive (MiFID II).

3. Greater focus on investor protection: The Madoff scandal helped to highlight the need for greater investor protection measures, including stronger disclosure requirements, clearer investor education, and more robust enforcement mechanisms.

4. Increased skepticism among investors: The Madoff scandal also contributed to increased skepticism among investors, who became more wary of investment opportunities that seemed too good to be true. This increased skepticism has had both positive and negative effects, as it has helped to prevent some investors from falling prey to scams, but has also made it more difficult for legitimate investment opportunities to attract funding.

5. Improved fraud detection and prevention measures: The Madoff scandal helped to spur improvements in fraud detection and prevention measures, as financial institutions and regulators worked to develop new tools and strategies for identifying and preventing fraudulent activity.

Overall, the Madoff scandal was a wake-up call for the financial industry, regulators, and investors, highlighting the need for greater transparency, accountability, and investor protection measures. While the scandal had devastating consequences for Madoff's victims, it also helped to spur positive changes within the financial industry and contributed to a more robust and resilient financial system.

BEAR STEARNS MORTGAGE-BACKED SECURITIES SCANDAL (2008)

The Bear Stearns Mortgage-Backed Securities Scandal was a financial crisis that occurred in 2008, which resulted in the bankruptcy of one of the largest investment banks in the United States, Bear Stearns. The scandal was a significant contributor to the global financial crisis that began in 2008 and had far-reaching effects on the financial industry and the global economy.

Bear Stearns was a leading investment bank that specialized in mortgage-backed securities (MBS). The bank packaged home loans into securities that could be sold to investors. The securities were typically rated by credit rating agencies and were considered safe investments with a low risk of default.

However, the financial crisis that began in 2008 was fueled by a dramatic increase in subprime mortgages, which were home loans that were issued to borrowers with poor credit histories. Many of these loans were issued with adjustable interest rates that would increase significantly after a few years, making them unaffordable for many borrowers. As a result, many homeowners defaulted on their loans, causing the value of the mortgage-backed securities to plummet.

Bear Stearns had heavily invested in subprime mortgages and

had a large portfolio of mortgage-backed securities. When the value of these securities began to decline, the bank was left with significant losses. In March 2008, Bear Stearns announced that two of its hedge funds that had invested in subprime mortgages were facing significant losses, which caused its stock price to plummet.

The announcement triggered a run on the bank, with investors withdrawing their money from the bank. The Federal Reserve stepped in to provide emergency funding to the bank, but it was not enough to save the bank from bankruptcy. On March 16, 2008, Bear Stearns was acquired by JP Morgan Chase in a government-backed deal worth $10 per share, which was significantly lower than the bank's previous stock price.

1. 2003 - 2007: A significant increase in subprime mortgages occurs, with many borrowers receiving adjustable rate mortgages (ARMs) that would increase significantly after a few years.
2. 2006: Bear Stearns begins to experience significant losses due to its exposure to mortgage-backed securities.
3. 2007: Bear Stearns closes down two of its hedge funds that were heavily invested in subprime mortgages.
4. February 2008: The CEO of Bear Stearns, Alan Schwartz, reassures investors that the bank has a strong liquidity position.
5. March 2008: Two of Bear Stearns' hedge funds, which invested in subprime mortgages, suffer significant losses.
6. March 13, 2008: Bear Stearns announces that it is seeking emergency funding from the Federal Reserve and JPMorgan Chase.
7. March 14, 2008: The Federal Reserve announces that it will provide emergency funding to Bear Stearns.
8. March 16, 2008: JPMorgan Chase agrees to acquire Bear Stearns in a government-backed deal worth $10 per share, significantly lower than the bank's previous stock

price.

9. March 17, 2008: The New York Federal Reserve announces a plan to provide up to $200 billion in funding to banks to address the liquidity crisis.

The Bear Stearns scandal highlighted the significant risks associated with mortgage-backed securities and the dangers of investing in subprime mortgages. It also raised questions about the effectiveness of credit rating agencies, which had given high ratings to many of these securities despite their inherent risks.

The scandal had far-reaching effects on the financial industry and the global economy. It triggered a wave of bank failures and led to a severe recession that lasted for several years. Governments around the world were forced to intervene to prevent the collapse of their financial systems, and many countries experienced significant economic downturns.

The Bear Stearns Mortgage-Backed Securities Scandal of 2007-2008 was one of the major events that led to the global financial crisis of 2008. The scandal involved the sale and trading of subprime mortgage-backed securities that were packaged and sold to investors, including many banks and financial institutions. The securities were based on subprime mortgages, which were high-risk loans made to borrowers with poor credit histories and limited incomes.

The collapse of the subprime mortgage market and the subsequent decline in housing prices caused many borrowers to default on their loans, leading to massive losses for the banks and financial institutions that had invested in these securities. Bear Stearns, one of the largest players in the market, was hit particularly hard and was eventually forced to declare bankruptcy in March 2008.

The scandal had significant global implications and led to a number of regulatory changes aimed at preventing similar crises in the future. In the United States, the Dodd-Frank Wall Street Reform and Consumer Protection Act of 2010 was passed, which included measures to increase transparency and accountability in the financial industry, as well as new regulations on the trading of derivatives and the creation of a consumer protection agency.

Internationally, the scandal led to increased scrutiny of the financial industry and calls for greater regulation of the global financial system. The G20, a group of the world's largest economies, agreed to a number of reforms aimed at improving financial stability and preventing future crises. These included measures to increase transparency in the derivatives market, strengthen regulation of credit rating agencies, and improve the supervision of banks and other financial institutions.

Overall, the Bear Stearns Mortgage-Backed Securities Scandal had far-reaching consequences and led to significant regulatory changes in the financial industry. While these measures have helped to improve stability in the global financial system, many experts believe that more needs to be done to prevent future crises and protect consumers from the risks associated with complex financial products.

COUNTRYWIDE FINANCIAL MORTGAGE FRAUD SCANDAL (2007)

The Countrywide Financial Mortgage Fraud Scandal of 2007 was one of the largest financial scandals in the United States. Countrywide, a mortgage lender and servicer, was accused of engaging in fraudulent and predatory lending practices that contributed to the subprime mortgage crisis of 2008.

The scandal centered around the sale and securitization of subprime mortgages, which were high-risk loans made to borrowers with poor credit histories and limited incomes. Countrywide was one of the largest players in the subprime mortgage market, and it is estimated that the company originated or serviced over $1 trillion in mortgages between 2005 and 2007.

One of the key allegations against Countrywide was that it engaged in a practice known as "steering," in which the company directed borrowers to take out subprime loans even if they qualified for lower-cost prime loans. According to a lawsuit filed by the state of Illinois, Countrywide's "high-cost loan business model was built on deception, preying on vulnerable borrowers who were led to believe that they were getting better loans than they actually were."

Another allegation against Countrywide was that it engaged in widespread fraud in the sale and securitization of subprime mortgages. The company allegedly made false representations about the quality of the loans it was selling, including misrepresenting the borrowers' income, employment status, and credit history. These loans were then packaged and sold to investors as mortgage-backed securities, which contributed to the eventual collapse of the subprime mortgage market.

In 2008, Countrywide agreed to a $8.7 billion settlement with a group of state attorneys general, which included funding for loan modifications and other relief for borrowers. The settlement was the largest of its kind at the time.

1. Countrywide Financial Corporation, a mortgage lending company based in California, began offering subprime mortgages in the early 2000s. These loans were often made to borrowers with poor credit and high debt-to-income ratios.

2. Countrywide Financial encouraged its employees to sell as many mortgages as possible, even to borrowers who might not be able to afford them. Employees were given incentives to close loans quickly, without fully vetting the borrowers' financial status.

3. In order to make these subprime loans more attractive to investors, Countrywide Financial began bundling them together into complex financial instruments known as mortgage-backed securities (MBS). These MBS were then sold to investors, who were promised high returns on their investments.

4. Countrywide Financial also engaged in a practice known as "liar loans," in which borrowers were not required to provide documentation of their income or assets. This made it easier for Countrywide Financial to sell more loans, but it also increased the risk of default.

5. As the housing market began to decline in 2007, many of the borrowers who had taken out subprime mortgages from Countrywide Financial began to default

on their loans. This caused the value of the mortgage-backed securities to plummet, leading to significant losses for investors.

6. In 2008, Bank of America acquired Countrywide Financial for $4 billion. After the acquisition, Bank of America discovered evidence of widespread fraud and deception within Countrywide Financial, including the use of fraudulent documentation and the sale of mortgages to borrowers who were not qualified.

7. In 2010, Bank of America agreed to pay $108 million to settle a lawsuit brought by the Federal Trade Commission (FTC) over Countrywide Financial's practices. The settlement required Bank of America to provide refunds to affected borrowers and to implement new procedures to prevent future fraud.

Overall, the Countrywide Financial Mortgage Fraud Scandal involved a range of fraudulent and deceptive practices by a major mortgage lender, leading to significant losses for investors and borrowers alike.

The scandal also had broader implications for the financial industry and led to significant regulatory changes. In 2010, the Dodd-Frank Wall Street Reform and Consumer Protection Act was passed, which included measures to increase transparency and accountability in the financial industry, as well as new regulations on the trading of derivatives and the creation of a consumer protection agency.

The Countrywide Financial Mortgage Fraud Scandal was one of the major events that contributed to the global financial crisis of 2008. While the regulatory changes that followed have helped to improve stability in the financial industry, many experts believe that more needs to be done to prevent future crises and protect consumers from predatory lending practices.

WASHINGTON MUTUAL FAILURE (2008)

Washington Mutual, or WaMu, was a large financial institution based in Seattle, Washington that specialized in home lending, credit cards, and other consumer banking services. At its height, WaMu was the largest savings and loan association in the United States, with assets totaling more than $300 billion.

However, in the early 2000s, WaMu began to expand aggressively, making risky loans to borrowers with poor credit and offering subprime mortgages with adjustable interest rates. These loans were bundled together into mortgage-backed securities (MBS) and sold to investors, promising high returns.

As the housing market began to decline in 2007, many of the borrowers who had taken out subprime mortgages from WaMu began to default on their loans. This caused the value of the MBS to plummet, leading to significant losses for investors.

In addition to its exposure to the subprime mortgage market, WaMu also faced a number of internal problems. The company was plagued by a high rate of employee turnover, and many of its loan officers were accused of engaging in unethical or fraudulent practices to close loans quickly.

In 2008, WaMu's problems came to a head when it became clear that the company was insolvent and would not be able to repay its debts. In September of that year, federal regulators seized WaMu and placed it into receivership, making it the largest bank failure in U.S. history at the time.

The failure of WaMu had significant repercussions for the broader financial system. The FDIC, which insured the deposits of WaMu's customers, had to pay out more than $12 billion to depositors after the bank's collapse. In addition, the failure of WaMu and other financial institutions led to a severe credit crunch, making it difficult for businesses and consumers to access credit.

The failure of WaMu was also significant because it highlighted the role of regulators in overseeing the financial industry. In the aftermath of the financial crisis, many critics argued that regulators had failed to adequately supervise banks like WaMu, allowing them to engage in risky lending practices that ultimately led to their downfall.

Following its seizure by regulators, WaMu's assets were sold to JP Morgan Chase for $1.9 billion. JP Morgan Chase later settled a lawsuit brought by the FDIC over its acquisition of WaMu's assets, agreeing to pay $645 million in damages to the FDIC.

Overall, the failure of Washington Mutual was a significant event in the 2008 financial crisis, highlighting the risks of the subprime mortgage market and the importance of effective regulatory oversight in the financial industry.

LLOYDS BANKING GROUP PPI SCANDAL (2011)

The Payment Protection Insurance (PPI) scandal involved the mis-selling of insurance products by banks and other financial institutions in the UK. PPI was sold to customers as a way to protect against defaulting on loans, credit cards, and other forms of debt. However, many of these policies were sold to customers who did not need or want them, or who were not eligible to claim on them.

One of the largest banks involved in the PPI scandal was Lloyds Banking Group, which includes the brands Lloyds Bank, Halifax, and Bank of Scotland. Lloyds had a significant share of the UK's PPI market, with around 40% of all PPI policies sold in the UK between 2005 and 2010.

In 2011, an investigation by the Financial Conduct Authority (FCA) found that Lloyds had engaged in widespread mis-selling of PPI to its customers. The FCA found that Lloyds had used high-pressure sales tactics to sell PPI, and that many of its employees had been incentivized to sell as many policies as possible, without fully explaining the terms and conditions to customers.

In addition to mis-selling PPI, Lloyds was also found to have mishandled PPI claims from its customers. The FCA found that Lloyds had rejected many valid claims, and that it had failed to provide adequate compensation to customers who had been mis-sold PPI.

As a result of the PPI scandal, Lloyds was forced to pay out billions of pounds in compensation to its customers. By 2018, Lloyds had paid out more than £20 billion in PPI compensation, making it the largest compensation scheme in UK history.

The PPI scandal also had significant repercussions for the wider banking industry in the UK. The scandal led to a loss of trust in the banking sector, and it prompted the FCA to introduce new regulations aimed at preventing the mis-selling of financial products in the future.

In addition to the financial costs of the scandal, the PPI scandal also damaged Lloyds' reputation and led to significant changes in the way the bank operates. Following the scandal, Lloyds implemented a number of reforms aimed at improving its culture and governance, including the appointment of a new CEO and the creation of a dedicated team to handle PPI claims.

Overall, the Lloyds Banking Group PPI scandal was a significant event in the history of the UK banking industry, highlighting the risks of mis-selling financial products and the importance of effective regulation and oversight. The scandal led to significant financial costs for Lloyds and other banks, and it prompted a renewed focus on consumer protection in the financial sector.

UBS ROGUE TRADER SCANDAL (2011)

The UBS rogue trader scandal refers to a series of unauthorized trades made by Kweku Adoboli, a trader at Swiss bank UBS, that resulted in losses of $2.3 billion in 2011. Adoboli was a trader on the bank's Delta One desk, which traded in equities, futures, and options.

Adoboli's trading strategy involved making large bets on the direction of the market, using complex financial instruments such as exchange-traded funds (ETFs) and futures contracts. He concealed his trades by creating fictitious hedges and booking them as fictitious trades, which allowed him to exceed his trading limits without detection.

1. Adoboli's trading strategy involved making large bets on the direction of the market, using complex financial instruments such as exchange-traded funds (ETFs) and futures contracts.

2. Adoboli concealed his trades by creating fictitious hedges and booking them as fictitious trades, which allowed him to exceed his trading limits without detection.

3. Adoboli initially made small, profitable trades to build up his reputation and gain the trust of his superiors at UBS.

4. Adoboli then began to take bigger risks, which resulted in large losses for the bank.

5. In an attempt to conceal his losses, Adoboli booked fake

trades and created fictitious hedges.

6. Adoboli's fraudulent activities were uncovered by UBS in September 2011, after he attempted to conceal losses by booking fake trades.

7. Adoboli was arrested and charged with fraud and false accounting, and was later sentenced to seven years in prison.

8. The scandal resulted in losses of $2.3 billion for UBS.

9. The scandal exposed weaknesses in UBS's risk management and internal controls, as well as the need for greater regulation and oversight of the banking industry.

10. In the aftermath of the scandal, UBS launched an internal review of its risk management processes and controls, and implemented a number of reforms aimed at preventing similar incidents in the future.

11. The scandal had broader implications for the banking industry as a whole, raising questions about the effectiveness of risk management and the culture of the banking industry.

The fraud was uncovered by UBS in September 2011, after Adoboli attempted to conceal losses by booking fake trades. Adoboli was arrested and charged with fraud and false accounting, and was later sentenced to seven years in prison.

The UBS rogue trader scandal was a major embarrassment for the bank, which had only recently recovered from a previous scandal involving tax evasion by its clients. The scandal also highlighted the weaknesses in UBS's risk management and internal controls, as well as the need for greater regulation and oversight of the banking industry.

In the aftermath of the scandal, UBS launched an internal review of its risk management processes and controls, and implemented a number of reforms aimed at preventing similar incidents in the future. The bank also faced regulatory fines and legal action from investors who had suffered losses as a result of the scandal.

The UBS rogue trader scandal had broader implications for the banking industry as a whole, as it raised questions about the effectiveness of risk management and the culture of the banking industry. The scandal prompted calls for greater transparency and accountability in the financial sector, and led to a renewed focus on risk management and internal controls across the industry.

The incident revealed a number of breakdowns in risk management controls at UBS, including:

1. Inadequate oversight: There was a lack of oversight of Adoboli's trading activities, which allowed him to make unauthorized trades over a period of several years. UBS did not have adequate controls in place to monitor Adoboli's trades or to prevent him from exceeding his authorized risk limits.

2. Weak risk management framework: The bank's risk

management framework was weak and ineffective, with insufficient controls to detect and prevent fraudulent activity. There was also a lack of segregation of duties, which allowed Adoboli to execute trades and then hide them from the bank's risk management team.

3. Poor communication: There was poor communication between UBS's front and back offices, which allowed Adoboli to circumvent controls and execute unauthorized trades. The bank's risk management team was not informed of the trades until after the losses had occurred, which prevented them from taking action to prevent further losses.

4. Ineffective compliance function: The bank's compliance function was ineffective in detecting and preventing fraudulent activity. Adoboli was able to circumvent the bank's compliance processes by falsifying records and hiding his trades.

Overall, the UBS rogue trader scandal was a significant event in the history of the banking industry, highlighting the need for stronger risk management processes and controls, as well as the importance of greater transparency and accountability in the financial sector.

RBS GLOBAL RESTRUCTURING GROUP SCANDAL (2013)

The RBS Global Restructuring Group (GRG) scandal was a financial scandal that occurred in 2013 involving the Royal Bank of Scotland (RBS) and its GRG division, which was responsible for managing troubled loans. The scandal involved allegations of widespread mistreatment of small business customers, including forced loan default, inappropriate fees, and asset stripping.

The GRG division was created in response to the 2008 financial crisis, and it was designed to help small business customers who were struggling with their loans. However, instead of providing assistance, the division was accused of exploiting the customers for profit.

The scandal first came to light in 2013 when an internal report by RBS was leaked to the media. The report alleged that the GRG division had engaged in widespread mistreatment of small business customers, including forcing them into default so that the bank could seize their assets. The report also alleged that the division had charged inappropriate fees and imposed punitive interest rates.

The scandal led to a number of investigations by UK regulatory authorities, including the Financial Conduct Authority (FCA) and the Prudential Regulation Authority (PRA). The FCA conducted a review of the GRG division and found that there had been widespread mistreatment of small business customers. The FCA also found that the division had failed to provide appropriate support and that the bank had not acted in the best interests of its customers.

As a result of the scandal, RBS set aside £400 million to compensate affected customers. However, many of the customers have criticized the compensation process, claiming that it has been slow and inadequate.

The scandal has also led to significant reputational damage for RBS, which is still struggling to rebuild its reputation. In addition, it has led to calls for greater regulation of the banking sector and for greater protection for small business customers.

Bucks by Caryibuies

In conclusion, the RBS GRG scandal was a significant financial scandal that highlighted the need for greater regulation of the banking sector and for greater protection for small business customers. The scandal led to significant reputational damage for RBS and has had a lasting impact on the banking industry.

RABOBANK LIBOR SCANDAL (2013)

The Rabobank Libor scandal was a major financial scandal that occurred in 2013 and involved the Dutch cooperative bank, Rabobank. The scandal centered around the bank's manipulation of the London Interbank Offered Rate (Libor), which is a benchmark interest rate that banks use to price loans and financial instruments.

Rabobank was one of several major banks that were accused of manipulating Libor during the period from 2005 to 2010. The bank was accused of colluding with other banks to manipulate the rate in order to benefit its trading positions and to enhance its profits. The bank was also accused of submitting false and misleading information to Libor in order to manipulate the rate.

Here are the steps by which Rabobank manipulated the LIBOR:

1. Submitting false LIBOR rates: Rabobank traders manipulated the LIBOR rates by submitting false rates that were not based on actual transactions. They did this to influence the final LIBOR rate and benefit their own trading positions.

2. Coordinating with other banks: Rabobank traders colluded with traders from other banks to manipulate the LIBOR rate. They would submit false rates to each other, which would then be used to influence the final LIBOR rate.

3. Suppressing rates: Rabobank traders also suppressed

LIBOR rates in order to make their borrowing costs appear lower than they actually were. This helped the bank appear more financially stable than it actually was.

4. Threatening colleagues: Some Rabobank traders threatened colleagues who refused to take part in the manipulation of LIBOR rates. These threats helped to maintain the culture of collusion and allowed the manipulation to continue unchecked.

Overall, the manipulation of LIBOR by Rabobank was a complex and coordinated effort involving multiple traders and spanning several years. The bank's actions not only undermined the integrity of the LIBOR benchmark, but also violated the trust of customers and the wider public.

In November 2013, Rabobank reached a settlement with US and European regulators in which it agreed to pay a total of $1.07 billion in fines and penalties. This was one of the largest ever settlements in a Libor-related case.

The scandal had significant consequences for Rabobank, which had been known for its conservative and ethical approach to banking. The bank's reputation was severely damaged by the scandal, and it was forced to make major changes to its management and compliance practices. Rabobank's CEO and CFO both resigned in the wake of the scandal.

The scandal also had wider implications for the banking industry. The manipulation of Libor by banks was seen as evidence of a broader culture of unethical behavior within the industry. The scandal led to calls for greater regulation and oversight of the banking sector and for tougher penalties for banks that engage in illegal or unethical behavior. It also led to a loss of public trust in the banking sector, which has had lasting effects.

Since the scandal, Rabobank has implemented a number of measures to improve its compliance and risk management practices. The bank has increased its investment in compliance and has hired additional staff to oversee its operations. It has also implemented stricter controls on its Libor submissions and has strengthened its internal controls and governance structures.

In conclusion, the Rabobank Libor scandal was a significant financial scandal that had significant consequences for the bank and for the banking industry as a whole. The scandal highlighted the need for greater transparency and accountability in the banking industry, and it led to calls for tougher penalties for banks that engage in illegal or unethical behavior. Rabobank has taken steps to address the issues that led to the scandal, but the effects of the scandal continue to be felt in the industry.

The financial world has moved from LIBOR-based curves to risk-free rates (RFRs) and the relationship to the LIBOR scandal:

1. Lack of trust in LIBOR: The LIBOR scandal in 2012-13 highlighted the potential for manipulation of benchmark interest rates, which eroded trust in LIBOR. This, in turn, led to a need for alternative benchmark rates that were less susceptible to manipulation.

2. Regulatory scrutiny: Following the LIBOR scandal, regulators began to scrutinize the LIBOR benchmark more closely and imposed stricter requirements for its calculation and reporting. This increased regulatory scrutiny led to greater uncertainty and volatility in LIBOR-based markets, making them less attractive to market participants.

3. Inadequate underlying transactions: The LIBOR benchmark was based on interbank lending transactions, which had become less frequent and less reliable in the years following the financial crisis. This led to concerns about the accuracy and reliability of LIBOR as a benchmark rate.

4. Changes in market dynamics: The LIBOR benchmark was traditionally used to price a wide range of financial instruments, including loans, bonds, and derivatives. However, changes in market dynamics, such as the growth of the swaps market, made LIBOR less relevant as a benchmark rate.

5. Development of alternative RFRs: In response to the concerns about LIBOR, regulators and market participants began to develop alternative RFRs that were based on actual transactions and less susceptible to manipulation. These new RFRs, such as the Secured Overnight Financing Rate (SOFR) in the US and the Sterling Overnight Index Average (SONIA) in the UK, have been gradually adopted by market participants as a replacement for LIBOR.

In summary, the LIBOR scandal undermined trust in the

benchmark rate and led to regulatory scrutiny, which in turn made LIBOR-based markets less attractive. Changes in market dynamics and the development of alternative RFRs further reduced the relevance of LIBOR as a benchmark rate, leading to the adoption of new RFRs by market participants.

COMMERZBANK MONEY LAUNDERING SCANDAL (2020)

In September 2020, Commerzbank, a major German bank, was hit with a €41 million ($47 million) fine by German regulators for failures in its anti-money laundering controls. The fine was the result of an investigation into the bank's processing of suspicious transactions between 2010 and 2015, which involved around 600 clients and €200 million ($230 million) worth of transactions.

The investigation found that Commerzbank had not taken sufficient measures to prevent money laundering and had not properly assessed the risks associated with certain clients and transactions. In some cases, the bank had failed to obtain necessary information about the origin of funds or the ultimate beneficiaries of transactions.

The bank was also found to have ignored warnings from its own anti-money laundering team and to have failed to report suspicious transactions to the relevant authorities. The investigation found that the bank had not implemented the necessary measures to detect and prevent such transactions and had not properly trained its staff in anti-money laundering procedures.

Commerzbank's CEO, Martin Zielke, resigned in July 2020, following criticism of his handling of the bank's strategy and performance. The money laundering scandal was seen as a major factor in his departure.

The fine imposed on Commerzbank was one of the largest ever levied by German regulators for anti-money laundering failures. The bank has since committed to improving its anti-money laundering controls and to implementing a number of remedial measures.

The scandal was seen as another blow to the reputation of the banking industry, which has been hit by a number of high-profile money laundering cases in recent years. It also highlighted the need for banks to take their anti-money laundering obligations seriously and to ensure that their systems and processes are effective in detecting and preventing financial crime.

BNP PARIBAS SCANDAL (2014)

In 2014, BNP Paribas, one of the largest banks in Europe, was fined $9 billion by US authorities for violating US sanctions against Iran, Sudan, and Cuba. The case was one of the largest financial settlements in US history and highlighted the importance of compliance with international sanctions regulations.

The investigation found that BNP Paribas had knowingly and intentionally violated US sanctions by processing transactions worth billions of dollars for clients in these countries between 2002 and 2012. The bank had deliberately concealed the true nature of these transactions and had used complex methods to evade detection by US regulators.

The US authorities alleged that BNP Paribas had employed several tactics to avoid detection, including using "stripped" payment messages that removed references to sanctioned countries, and employing third-party banks to process transactions on their behalf.

The case also highlighted the role of the US dollar in international transactions, with the majority of the transactions in question having been processed in US dollars. As a result, US authorities were able to claim jurisdiction over the case, despite BNP Paribas being a French bank.

1. Between 2002 and 2012, BNP Paribas processed billions of dollars in transactions for clients in Iran, Sudan, and Cuba, in violation of US sanctions against these

countries.

2. In 2007, BNP Paribas became aware that its US operations were processing transactions in violation of US sanctions, but the bank did not take sufficient action to address the issue.

3. In 2010, the US Department of Justice began investigating BNP Paribas for possible violations of US sanctions.

4. In 2012, BNP Paribas announced that it had set aside $1.1 billion to cover potential fines related to the US sanctions investigation.

5. In May 2014, BNP Paribas pleaded guilty to one count of violating US sanctions and agreed to pay a $9 billion fine, one of the largest fines in US history.

6. The US authorities alleged that BNP Paribas had employed several tactics to avoid detection, including using "stripped" payment messages that removed references to sanctioned countries, and employing third-party banks to process transactions on their behalf.

7. The settlement also included a five-year ban on conducting certain dollar-clearing transactions and the dismissal of several senior executives at the bank.

8. The scandal had a significant impact on BNP Paribas' reputation and financial performance, with the bank reporting a significant drop in profits in the months following the settlement.

9. The case highlighted the risks of non-compliance with international sanctions regulations and underscored the need for banks to take their compliance obligations seriously.

The $9 billion settlement was the result of a coordinated effort by US authorities, including the Department of Justice, the Federal Reserve, and the New York State Department of Financial Services. The settlement included a $140 million fine from the New York

State Department of Financial Services and a five-year ban on conducting certain dollar-clearing transactions.

The scandal had a significant impact on BNP Paribas' reputation and financial performance, and the bank was forced to take significant measures to improve its compliance controls and to rebuild trust with customers and investors.

The case also had broader implications for the international banking industry, highlighting the risks of non-compliance with international sanctions regulations and the potential consequences of evading detection by regulators. It underscored the need for banks to take their compliance obligations seriously and to ensure that their systems and processes are effective in detecting and preventing financial crime.

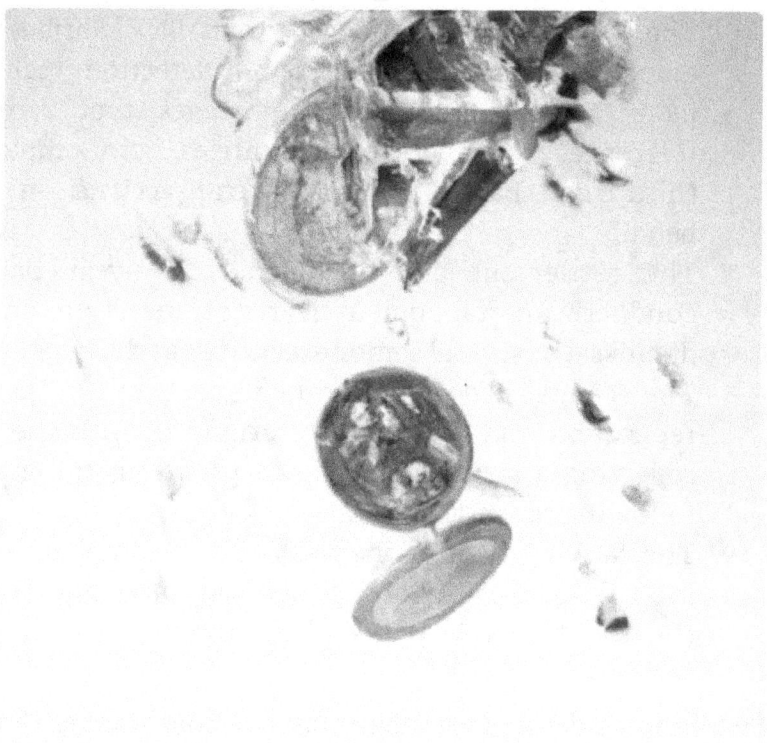

In conclusion, the BNP Paribas financial scandal of 2014 was a significant case that highlighted the importance of compliance with international sanctions regulations and the potential consequences of non-compliance. The case also underscored the need for banks to take their compliance obligations seriously and to ensure that their systems and processes are effective in detecting and preventing financial crime.

www.ingramcontent.com/pod-product-compliance
Lightning Source LLC
Chambersburg PA
CBHW070748220526
45467CB00018B/1231